# I HOPE
# YOU WILL BE
# VERY HAPPY

Leadership Lessons From A Lifetime In Lacrosse

# I Hope You Will Be Very Happy

### Leadership Lessons From A Lifetime In Lacrosse

## DOM STARSIA

Creator's Game Books
Baltimore
2019

Creator's Game Books
132-B Industry Lane, Unit #7
Forest Hill, MD 21050
http://www.cemeterydance.com


Trade Paperback Edition Printing


ISBN: 978-1-58767-760-1


Cover Photo © 2014 by Evan Vosburgh
Interior Design © 2019 by Desert Isle Design, LLC

Creator's Game Books is an imprint
of Cemetery Dance Publications

To Krissy, Molly, Joe, Maggie and Emma and now...
Pam, Dom and Weeg
To my brothers and sisters
To all the coaches, trainers, staff people, the parents
To my teammates
And especially to all the players...
"I have been blessed beyond words"

May 30, 2011…

Having beaten Denver in the semifinals, we're now in the NCAA D1 Championship game against a familiar ACC foe, the University of Maryland. They clobbered us on our home field earlier, our watershed low point in a trying regular season. Our man-to-man defense could not keep up with their potent scorers and we had lost our most experienced defensive player midway through that first game and for the rest of the season. In hindsight, we can thank the Terps for pointing out our weaknesses. At the same time, if the Terps were even slightly overconfident from the decisive outcome of this earlier game, we might be able to use this to our advantage.

The weatherman predicted temperatures in the mid 90s with high humidity adding double digit degrees to the heat index. In fact, on the field it registered 120 degrees during the game. I do not remember ever being hotter. The heat waves coming off the stadium field gave the crowd a surreal view of the action, making it even more of a spectacle. But the heat didn't blur the importance of our staying in the moment, and "getting this done." Earlier that morning, the ESPN announcers, Sean McDonough and Quint Kessenich, had asked if they could broadcast my pre-game speech. I told them, "I'm no Knute Rockne, but sure."

In the locker room, my routine is simply to pace anxiously. Back in 1999, Tucker Radebaugh had said to me that the team needed rousing pre-game speeches and I put some more time into it for that group. Doing that is part of the fun of college sports, sticking your neck out a little bit to try and lift the team. There is no doubt in my mind that the results of these games are much more determined in the days, weeks, months and even the years that precede these climactic moments. Everything we have been through in these past years has had an influence on our preparation for this opening championship face-off. I trust our players and the journey that brought us to this moment.

The head coach does need to say something as the team is about to depart the locker room, and while I put some thought into what that might be, it never goes much beyond an outline of how to get started. I may have bellowed the following words to the team but they came from a quiet, private place and touched on many of the themes I try to stress every day:

Hey…Everybody's gotta prepare as if their role is the most important one…

It's gonna be the one that makes the difference in this game…

That's what we gotta have right there…

We only do this if we do it together as a group…

We need the power of the group more than anything else…

Everybody right on top of this thing…

This is just the perfect day out there for us…

This is just what we needed…

We always thought about doing this…

This is always where we wanted to be...

It's coming up just the way we wanted it to be right
there...

A little smile on your face, a little joy in your heart...

Knowing that you are prepared, you've paid the price...

Now make it happen out there...

Let's finish this thing on the field...

We've been together through all of this year, working our
butt off the whole time...

Let's make this happen right now...

Bend your back...

Put your hand on the plastic of your stick...

Get the ball up off the ground...

All those things, they still make the big differences...

Move your feet...

Open your mouth...

Take care of each other out there in every instance, OK?...

Move yourself without it on offense...

Clear the space so you can clear your hands every time...

Hey, WHY NOT US?...

LET'S DO THIS...

1-2-3 TEAM!!!

We became the lowest seeded team, with the most regular season losses in history to win this 2011 National Championship. While those are the obvious facts, there is no simple way to describe this 2011 season. I cannot talk with anyone, trying to describe the events that led to this Championship, without waxing philosophic. I have been doing this a long time, I thought I had most of it figured out..."there is no divine intervention in athletics…you may play with character but, most everybody does…do you really 'love' your teammates?" What we had just gone through turned my world upside down. With everything that we had had to endure, I believe the winning became less important. I was getting a lot of credit for the grand scheme of how it all unfolded but there were many times throughout the spring that I was simply trying to get to the next day. Having lived through some of the events that forever changed our lives, I found myself drawing some comfort knowing that the principle of "what is the right thing to do here?" was my most consistent standard. Never mind my barking in the locker room before we went onto the field…the last thing I told the team at the pre-game meal the morning of the championship was "in the end, whether or not we win today is less important than how we treat people."

In this instance, for this team, it sure did seem as if someone was watching out for us, that we had faced enough adversity to qualify for truly having defined our character (that had nothing to do with the scores of these games) and that getting close enough to the essence of each other is probably what love is all about. I am so appreciative that I was able to experience that 2011 season. It was never easy but, it sure was worth it.

# INTRODUCTION

---

The title of this book is the subtle response of my wife to an innocent comment I had made about hearing earlier in the day that Jim Adams, the head lacrosse coach at the University of Virginia, was retiring at the end of that 1992 season. She may have had a sixth sense but I truly do not remember having spent one moment that day considering the possibility of a move to Charlottesville. Krissy and I had met at Brown, spent 22 years in Providence, our four children were born there, I loved coaching at my alma mater, and we were ingrained in the community. However, the "best laid plans" get changed and the 2018-19 academic year will be our 27th in Virginia. With my dad, two brothers and their families, my mother in law, two brothers in law, three nephews and a niece at UVA, Starsia's and Lasagna's alike, all having followed us to town, we probably doubled the Italian-American population in this sleepy southern hamlet.

I have been encouraged to write a story about my life in lacrosse and I continue to consider that possibility. What I have decided, however, is an attempt to offer a more practical handbook for coaches, players, fans and parents. While most of these essays have previously been published, many have been revised and updated. I hope that what you may find most useful is having them all centrally located.

I believe it may have been Hunter Thompson who was paraphrasing Mark Twain when he said, "The difference between a good choice in a word and the perfect choice in a word is the difference between lightning and a lightning bug." I have often used that quote while talking to my team about attention to detail, the quality of preparation, how the little things make a big difference, etc. I harbor no illusions about penning the "perfect word" in this attempt to offer some guidance about one man's life in lacrosse. While being interviewed for the head coaching position at the University of Virginia, one of the people on the committee asked me to define myself. I hesitated for a second, then replied simply, "I'm honest and I'll work hard." The compilation of these essays follows the same guidelines.

To all my former assistant coaches and players, I am sorry that I could not include all of your pictures, because none of this happens without your contributions and your influence on my life and career. I have inserted some of my favorite maxims throughout the text, especially in the "Lacrosse" section. I often used them to set a tone for practice, a week's preparation, or an opening thought for pre-game remarks.

Since having walked away from coaching at UVA following the spring of 2016, I have become more involved as an Executive Board member of Harlem Lacrosse, chair the "Champion the Game" committee for the Intercollegiate Men's Lacrosse Coaches Committee, served as the chair for US Lacrosse's National Hall of Fame committee, am the Head Coach for Team Chrome in the inaugural season of the Premier Lacrosse League, have written most of these essays and have met with men's and women's coaching staffs and teams at all levels. At times, I imagine that I may be overcompensating for a concern that I still have something to offer. I ran across a quote by Picasso recently that seems to speak to me, not solely, but directly: "The meaning of life is to find your gift. The purpose of life is to give it away." I hope that you will find something in these essays that helps you on your own path.

Picture on National Hall of Fame plaque after beating Johns Hopkins 2004

# TABLE OF CONTENTS

# LETTERS

# 1

## Letter to a College Freshman

*After ten years coaching college lacrosse and with two kids (Lil' Dom and Luigi) in tow, my 34 year old son is about to start Law School at the University of Texas come September (2017). His bold career choice reminds me that it just seems like yesterday when he began his undergraduate career at Lynchburg College. I would like to share with all the young men and women about to start their college careers a letter "I wish" I had sent to Joe...*

My son Joe looking over my shoulder

Dear Joe,

You are about to embark on a great adventure. In the grand scheme that is your life, I do not believe there will be a lot of other moments that have as profound an influence on your evolution as going away from home for the first time. It was the American poet E E Cummings who said "it takes courage to grow up and become who you really are" and I am confident you will exhibit that quality over these next four years. My concern, at this moment, is that the world has become less patient and forgiving and that you don't self-inflict too much pain and anguish especially in the early stages of this journey.

You have been around college lacrosse players your entire life. While I appreciate that we all need to experience situations firsthand in order to process them fully, I would hope that you have been listening to me tell generations of young men that "smart guys don't learn from their own mistakes, they learn from others'." I would be happy to provide you the contact information for any number of guys whose names you will recognize and who dug themselves a hole that they almost could not get out of. Don't make your life harder than it needs to be.

Along these lines, manage yourself with the guiding principle of "all things in moderation." You may not be looking at the first beer of your life but learn to say "enough," even when surrounded by upperclass mayhem. It may require a little leap of faith but I swear that these same teammates will come to respect you more in the daylight hours. It is the guys who speak with an uncompromising voice of reason who become the leaders on these teams.

Do you want to know the absolute key to success in the classroom and on the lacrosse field? Go to class and follow the

"Poskay Rule"...get up for breakfast every morning. If your commitment is to get up and eat something before 9:00am EVERY morning, I can almost guarantee that you will be fine in school and perform close to your potential as a college athlete. That's what you want, right?

If you are up in the morning, you will likely be presented with an opportunity to talk with some classmates who are not lacrosse players. Make that a daily goal. I am sure you are going to have wonderful teammates but don't limit your personal interactions to the guys you will be with for 4-5 hours a day, even if you want to. These other encounters will require you to consider events and situations outside the world of athletics.

Arrive on campus in shape and ready to compete. You will get one chance to make a first impression. What do you want the coaches to think of you? Strive to be first in the early conditioning, don't be last.

Tell the truth, always. Don't compromise here, lying always requires more lying and it is a slippery slope. Whether you are talking to a teacher, an academic advisor, your coach, your friends or, looking in the mirror, take responsibility for your life and actions. If something goes astray, square up and face the music... it will always give you the best chance to move on.

Finally, stop calling your mother! I do not mean, literally, to stop calling your mother but I absolutely do mean that your parents don't have to hear about every time you stub your toe, every time the coach leaves you out of a drill or puts you on the second extra man. I also mean that your parents do not have to hear about mistakes that your teammates may have made, on or off the field. Part of being on a real team is keeping things within that team. It is hard enough to make things work smoothly with a group of 45 college age young men (and women) without the additional hurtfulness that accompanies gossip and social media. This one is about growing up and being out on your own, about being part of a group that is on a special mission and about cherishing the privacy of that commitment.

Joe, if that seems like a lot, believe me, I'm jealous…I wish it was me.

Love,
Dad

# 2

## Letter to Parents

Dear Parents,

I have been meaning to write this letter for some time. This coming 2006 season will be my 32nd as a fulltime college lacrosse coach. It will also be my final one as the parent of a college athlete. I have been blessed in my career to have worked at two of the finest academic institutions in the country. There have been so many wonderful families and athletes that I have come to know over the years. Many remain as close friends. My daughter Molly started in the field hockey goal for Columbia University between 1999 and 2002 and my son, Joe, is presently a senior defenseman at Lynchburg College. I stand on the sidelines for a living and sit among the parents at every possible opportunity. I would like to try and present some perspective on the often misunderstood relationship between the two.

Let's start with the recruiting…it would be immature and shortsighted for a coach to "guarantee" that your son or daughter will be an immediate starter, or guarantee that another young prospect will start over your child. As a coach, it is a base requirement to make every candidate and their family welcome during the recruiting. As a parent, you need to be savvy enough to understand that this process is a predictive, inexact science, at best. Coaches may certainly imply that a certain sequence of events is likely to happen, but playing time is determined on the practice field. When we recruited two goalies in the same class a few years back, the "second" candidate considered his decision and asked simply, "Will I get a fair chance when I get there?" I assured him that there were 36 other young men who had a vested interest in determining the starting goalie.

My son made the final choice to go to Lynchburg College. My wife and I were comfortable with the coach (very comfortable with Steve Koudelka) and the institution, but Joe was the one who would be making his way and living with the daily consequences. I read once that "you become a man the day you leave home." I try and support my son in every way that I can. But I sent him away to college to become a man and that includes his learning to deal with the joy and the heartaches that he will encounter along his journey.

College sports are a competitive enterprise—without seeing him in the weight room, the locker room, the practice field, etc. on a daily basis, I am in no position to comment on the evolution of a coach's decision that determines his playing time on game day. I believe I do understand how difficult it is to watch your son struggle with his athletic experience. I hope you will understand that it is near impossible for a parent to make an objective observation of that situation. My son is not a starter at Lynchburg and during games, I find myself watching his movement on the bench at least as much as I follow the action on the field. We evaluate the event through the eyes of our child... coaches' decisions, right or wrong, are made to put the team in the best position to succeed.

A true story…a parent came up to me in the parking lot after a Virginia game and asked if he could have a word. We had just beaten UMass, were undefeated at the time and went on to win a national championship in May. When I said, "sure," the dad went on to say, "great game, the team looks great, can I make an unbiased observation?" Uh oh. He went on to make what could have been an incredibly astute observation—"you really need to develop your defensive depth"—if his son had not been the 4-5th defenseman on that team. Let your son grow up, bite your tongue a little, encourage him to talk with the coach, tell him to work harder and play better.

The parents have an important role while the game is being played. They are the ambassadors for the program in the stands. I have witnessed the "lone wolf" parent who prefers the solitary stance off by himself and the other who "prowls" throughout; some sit quietly and some are more active participants. Whatever your persona, your behavior does make a difference. It is mildly amusing to hear the tone of personal indignation that accompanies the comments from the stands about rules interpretations and officiating. I hardly know all the rules of our game and, as far as I can tell, accuracy is not a requirement for this vociferous "expert."

More importantly, support the entire team, its performance and the coaching staff, in a positive way. We are all working toward the same end. We all want the team to win and play well. Negative comments make that outcome harder to attain. We had a timeout during a game, a few years back, when the players actually spent the first moments talking about a parent and "what the heck is he screaming about?" Here is a piece of advice that I have always tried to follow. Don't cheer for your own son by name. We know he is your son. We/he knows you love him. We all saw him make the same play. Use that opportunity to praise someone else in a more supportive role. Your son plays, mine may not. A little understated and unilateral encouragement is classy and makes a lot of friends.

Finally, the post-game tailgates...the ability of parents to make folding tables, Gatorade and Italian subs appear in an asphalt parking lot within minutes of a game's final whistle suggests to me that the story of the "loaves and the fishes" may have actually been about the first tailgate. When immediately following a game is generally one of the few times in my life when I am not prepared to eat, it has always been more about the fellowship of this event. Let's not lose that in an attempt to get "bigger and better." Everyone should feel welcome. This may or may not be a revelation to parents, but your sons are anxious to move on to their own post-game activities. Try and keep the athletic politics to a minimum. If you find a coaching staff hesitant to attend, make sure their spouses and children are included—the coaches will follow. After ignoring events at home for most of the week, we are looking to make up some ground.

I hope this is helpful. Let's enjoy a terrific spring...Go Lynchburg!

Dom Starsia

# 3

# Letter to Parents #2

2015

Dear Parents,

Hello again...I wrote to you previously nine years ago, when I tried to describe the relationship between a parent and his son's college lacrosse coach. I received enough encouraging feedback to attempt to address an issue that has grown exponentially in our sport during this period of time since: the role of the club program in your son's development and his recruiting at the college level.

There seems quite a bit of anguish and misconception surrounding this topic in the lacrosse community. Let me begin by saying that one of my chief concerns over the growth of the club system is that it would certainly seem to favor those who have the means to participate. Those who can afford to join the most expensive club program and meet all the affiliated costs of equipment, travel, tournament fees, etc., clearly have an advantage over those who cannot afford this same exposure. When you combine that with the availability of repeating a year and/or moving to a private school, those expenses and subsequent advantages become considerable and obvious.

While I believe the demographic for participation in our game has slowly begun to broaden and diversify, many of the club programs would seem a reach back to unfortunate stereotypes. There is also a lot of good that has accompanied the growth of the club programs, especially for those players in more remote and emerging areas. When the best players in an area gravitate to a club team, they may easily be exposed to a higher caliber of play than they find at their high school. If there is only a limited number of qualified coaches in an area, those same players now benefit from being able to work with them. Finally and primarily, the club teams generally have greater flexibility than the high school teams to provide outlets for more lacrosse—summer, fall, winter, indoor, etc. On balance, there is no question that a young player is going to benefit from having a stick in his hands and being exposed to the game more often.

While acknowledging these benefits, I would like to immediately address an issue that has begun to emerge. I may only be speaking to my own bias, but I absolutely wince when a young player tells me that he is giving up football or soccer to "concentrate" in lacrosse. You develop a deeper fundamental understanding of the team concepts involved in the sport of men's lacrosse on the football fields, soccer pitches, basketball courts and hockey rinks of your youth. You will be a better lacrosse player by playing other sports.

The qualities of toughness, teamwork, selflessness and shared sacrifice are developed in the daily environment required by participation in high school sports. While participation on a club team is not devoid of these qualities, there is no question that the commitment simply is not the same. What is of grave concern is the rising number of recent questions from parents concerning club coaches who are encouraging their sons to forgo other sports so that they would be available for club tournaments.

OK, now I am going to backtrack a little on what I just said. For the purposes of recruiting , a young high school player may need to participate in a limited number of lacrosse events during the school year. The college coaches are identifying candidates for their talent pool during the late fall and winter months. Not appearing at all at a prospect day and/or a select tournament from September to March could affect someone's recruiting at any particular institution. What I suggest is someone going to meet with the high school football or soccer coach and telling him, "I am absolutely committed to our high school football team. At the same time, I am absolutely committed to going to college to play lacrosse. On our off day, on these two weekends, I need to play in this particular tournament." Some will be reasonable, some will not. Your son may now be learning to make important decisions for himself.

I have had high school lacrosse coaches calling recently to ask how the college coaches feel about a high school and a club team in the same tournament. It is not a question of competing against each other, but rather, the young high school player being put in the position of having to decide between one team or the other. If there is a choice that needs to be made, my personal preference would be to encourage someone to play with his high school teammates, first and foremost. These are the people you live with. I believe you will want to strengthen those relationships. What I would really like to see is the club programs institute a policy that allows/requires players to play with their high school teams in these settings. It would be a good-faith gesture by the clubs regarding a young man's responsibilities and loyalty to his high school.

Finally, how do you choose one club over another? No matter what some of the club coaches might tell you, the college coaches do not really care what club you play for. All we care about is, are you good enough? Now, one club or another might expose you to more and bigger tournaments, but a candidate can also disappear in those settings. If we have reason to think your son is good enough, all we really need to know is where and when he will be playing. We will do the rest. It doesn't matter whose fancy club jersey you may be wearing. Play well, stand out amongst your peers and, as Daniel Day Lewis exclaimed in *The Last of the Mohicans,* we will find you!

Identify a club team with a reputable coach, someone who will conduct some practices and coach your son in a reasonable manner. A club coach with no professional training and no accountability to a high school or NCAA organization need not be screaming at your son every moment.

Find a program whose practice and tournament schedule fits your own. I would hope that you do not feel the need to turn your world completely upside down while trying to get your son to every tournament being held. We actually witness these young men wear down when they are going constantly from one event to another. In addition, an 11 year old boy should be able to play with his buddies in a lacrosse event that may fall outside the parameters of his club commitment.

Finally, finally, find a program you can afford. You should not have to refinance the house to play club lacrosse, especially since no one can guarantee you that scholarship to Slam Dunk U.

Hope this is of some help.

# 4

## Letter to a Rising Sophomore

*This past summer, I wrote a letter to my son Joe as if he was about to start his first year of college. I gave him some advice that I wish I had given him as he was about to start his undergraduate experience at Lynchburg College in 2003. In reality, he is 34 years old and in the spring of his first year as a Law School student at the University of Texas. If this was his freshman spring, here is the letter I would be writing to him with three years to go.*

Dear Joe,

You have almost made it to the end of your first year of college and you are still standing. With a couple of months to go, please do not take anything for granted. There are a lot of distractions ahead in your first college spring while trying to balance the demands of a college lacrosse season. I hope you have decided not to pledge a fraternity this spring. I am not sure I appreciate the value of the Greek system under any circumstance but adding fraternity rush obligations to college athletics and your academic responsibilities is a troublesome mix. I am not sure a single player comes to mind who had a positive academic performance while pledging a fraternity. It can seem very important at this moment in your life, but you will quickly look back at the pressure to join and wonder about all the fuss. Look to your teammates and classmates for the friendships that will sustain you in the years ahead.

Somewhat along these same lines, I am sure the University has addressed the issue of sexual misconduct. If you were not paying close enough attention, let me be even more direct. Treating women with respect has always been the only proper standard and the order of the day. However, the rules that govern relationship behavior are now being written, re-written, evaluated and fluidly adjudicated on a daily basis. You need to be cautious and even more respectful in any of these situations. While only "yes" means yes, proper permission cannot be granted if there is any excessive use of alcohol involved. If you think I am overreacting, there were two instances in my last six months on the staff where players were accused of sexual misconduct. Both could have turned out much worse.

Sorry if I have come across as the stern parent, although that is exactly what I intended. With each passing day, you will find the people in positions of authority all around you to be less patient of your behavior. You will quickly come to be regarded and evaluated less and less as a naïve freshman. You are ready for a higher standard; it is simply time now to "answer the bell." You are a college lacrosse player, and most of the young people learning to play the game would trade places with you in a heartbeat. You are one of the "chosen ones" and with this opportunity comes the responsibility to act accordingly and look for opportunities to give back to the community. I am sure your team will be involved in meaningful community service activities. I am suggesting to you to go above and beyond. Look for quiet, notable ways to pay forward your good fortune. This world needs you desperately and the satisfaction you will feel from helping others will help you traverse the ups and downs, the wins and losses of the busy life of a college student athlete.

Let me suggest that you consider staying at school for at least one summer school session. I think we can afford it and you can work for the period of time before and after summer school. This will give you a chance to get ahead in your school work and spend six weeks in the weight room with your team strength coach. You are only going to be in college for four years and lacrosse has always been a very important part of your adult life. You need to look for ways to distinguish your effort from your teammates. I acknowledge that the job market is competitive and there is value in a low-paying internship. However, there is no shame in defining yourself as a lacrosse player and making an all-out effort to prepare yourself for the next college season. Do a good job in school overall, you will find a job.

Finally, it is time to be a player of consequence. You played a little more than most of your frosh classmates but playing in your first year is often a circumstance of necessity and good fortune. You now know how the process works, you may spend the summer in the weight room...now, seize the moment. I remember very distinctly early in the spring of my sophomore year being on the third midfield, we never got to shoot during drills, were never even really told the plays. I went to the head coach who gave me a bunch of double talk about "something." That very day I decided I had had enough, stopped being afraid and would no longer be denied. I think that it took me less than a week to move up to the first midfield. My point is to take responsibility for your own life and career. Stick your neck out, it's worth it.

Good luck Joe…it has been fun watching you on this journey.

Love,
Dad

...with Big Dom and Joe, 1991

# 5

## Letter to Returning College Players

June 1, 2018

Dear Returning College Players,

Except in those years when we won the very last game in the college season, this first week of summer elicited consistently strong feelings. I would almost always be anxious to get back to work, determined that next year would our year. We would be the one to ride and defend like Yale, get an early lead like Wesleyan and battle for sixty minutes like the Dukes of James Madison. I was convinced that our players certainly felt the same way and that nothing would get in the way of our pursuit of this goal. Over the course of a long summer, internships, summer school, the opinions of parents and friends, the start of a new academic year, the most committed players graduating and a new group coming on board would contribute to that singular focus losing some of its edge.

I am here to tell you that the decisions you make TODAY will have significant bearing on whether your 2019 season will have a different ending. One of the top college women's coaches told me recently that the James Madison women lifted 3x a week at 7:00 am throughout the season and did not miss a single session.

She also mentioned that she was not certain that her team was prepared to make the same commitment. How about your team? It is not just the question of working hard or harder. Our 1999 National Championship team is likely still the hardest working team of my extended career. At the same time, we won additional championships with teams that did not make the same effort. The question is "what does your team need to do?" It could be morning workouts or dedication in the weight room, physical conditioning, social behavior away from the locker room and/or group dynamics in the locker room, etc.

I have often spoken about the essence of this endeavor being a coach convincing his team and/or teammates convincing each other that it is worth whatever the sacrifices and commitments required for success. It will certainly require a brand of individual fearlessness to stand up in front of your teammates and describe an uncompromising journey ahead. Yes, it will seem hard, but hard reminds us that the task is special. If it wasn't hard everyone would be doing it. I can assure you that it will be facing up to the daunting mountain of anticipation that will occupy most of your time. My good friend, Hesiod, the Greek poet, wrote in 700 BC…"Badness you can get easily, in quantity: the road is smooth and it lives close by. But in front of excellence the immortal gods have put sweat, and long and steep is the way to it, and rough at first. But when you come to the top, then it is easy, even though it is hard."

That '99 Virginia team had to overcome 27 years of hearing how they were not tough enough to win. The willingness to work harder everyday and to engage in a complicated discussion to manage behavior away from the locker room proved to be the formula required of that team for success. No one knew that beforehand, however, and the commitments made in fall and winter could not guarantee a championship in spring. What it did was give us a chance. We fought through the decisions but I can still recall vividly in the parking lot after capturing the championship, senior defenseman Courtlend Weisleder saying to me, "that wasn't so hard!" While there may have been some momentary indecision about whether to hit him or hug him, his reaction is the essence of what I am trying to describe to you. The commitment comes first, then (maybe) the reward. You need to convince yourself and your teammates that this leap of faith is worth the risk. Do you have enough time between now and the climax of your season next May?…you have exactly the time you need, if you start today. Do it.

Have a safe and restful summer.
Coach Starsia

# 6

# Summer Musings...
# A Letter to High School Students

I saw a recent piece on HBO Real Sports about Tom Byers, an American soccer coach living and coaching in Japan. He has had great success with a primary emphasis on "possessing the ball" for young players. His contention is that all the other skills required for success in soccer are secondary to an inherent ability to possess the ball.

As I was watching, it occurred to me that my recurrent message to young players is about a singular skill in our sport that may be a base requirement for proficiency in all others. I have written about the value of being a good passer and feel even more strongly about it as I consider the topic. You can't help but learn to catch the ball with nuance if you improve your passing skills. You will become a better shooter if you can pass with touch and accuracy to a moving target, etc. I am not sure you can play lacrosse if not an effective passer and the very best players are excellent passers. In recent history, two of the dominant middies in the college game, Paul Rabil and Myles Jones, became more complete players in the second half of their undergraduate careers when they added a credible passing threat to a consistent ability to get their own shot.

I have a concern for young players who become preoccupied with MLL players, trick shots and shooting in excess of 100 MPH. Their pockets are too deep, they drop the head of their stick before they are able and some of these youngsters cannot hit the cage in a fastest shot contest from standing 2 yards in front of the goal. I tell those same players that if the contest was overhand passing accuracy, that Paul Rabil would also win that contest. I am going out on a limb here to suggest that Paul learned to master that fundamental first before dropping his hands sidearm to gain the leverage required to shoot 111 MPH. Learn to pass overhand, to follow through with your stick toward the target and the requisite footwork before you start dropping the head of your stick to win the fastest shot. Would you like to improve your chances of playing on Championship Weekend?...learn to be a great passer.

I was speaking to a young man from North Carolina who was asking for advice about being recruited. It would be fair to describe him as a late bloomer, someone who had a good junior year, from an emerging area and who now felt he had the ability to play at the next level. He wanted to know if he still had a chance to be recruited. I told him that the second we hung up the phone, he needed to compile a list of his top schools and write a letter to each of the coaches at those institutions. Easy enough for computer-savvy prospects to personalize each one (Please have someone proofread the first one to each school. I can't tell you how many letters start out with, "Coach Starsia, I am very interested in the University of Notre Dame!" It is not a deal breaker but careless.). Include some basic information—school, grades, test scores, high school coach, contact info for him, club team, summer schedule, name of your club coach and his contact info also. Try to avoid subjective descriptions like

"I'm very coachable" or "I will be a hard worker." The first indication to me that you may not be coachable is that you think you are. In addition, for someone who has only experienced the first few years of a high school career, I'm sorry but, you have no idea about hard work. You can avoid these areas completely or, if you must, try "I look forward to working with you and your staff" and/or "I would greatly look forward to being a member of your program."

I am always much more interested in hearing about your high school football, basketball, etc. exploits. "Wow, this young man was really good in this HS summer lacrosse tournament I watched and he is the starting tailback for the HS football team." That would be a much more reliable indicator that you are the caliber of athlete to play at the next level. I might rather come watch you play football than another lacrosse tournament in the fall. I tell parents all the time that the simplest way to determine whether your son can play at the highest level D1 schools is to answer this question, "Is your son one of the best athletes at his high school (period)?"

Include a highlight tape, if you have one. Three or four minutes is plenty long enough. Please consider who is listening when you pick out the accompanying music and put your best stuff at the beginning of the tape. I might not make it to the third minute if you haven't gotten my attention pretty quickly.

While I have never seen this young man (from NC) play, the answer to his question of whether he might still be recruited is answered with another question, "are you good enough?" If you/ he are, there are still lots of good college opportunities out there.

Have a great 4th of July and enjoy the rest of the summer.

7

# Open Letter to the Lacrosse Community

I am very proud of my two older children. They are both strong advocates for a number of social justice issues and I wish I had more of the courage of their convictions. My daughter Molly is in the final semester of the graduate Divinity School at Vanderbilt University while working fulltime for the state of Tennessee Higher Education Initiative coordinating college placement in the men's maximum security prison system. Joe has coached college lacrosse these past eleven years and will almost certainly be the oldest in his class when he starts Law School this coming September. When they (and my daughter-in-law Pam) asked me to write a letter to *Inside Lacrosse* in an attempt to raise awareness for Native American issues, especially surrounding the DAPL, I was quick to oblige.

I have had a special interest in the Native American roots of lacrosse from the first moment I was introduced to the game in the spring of 1971. I was a history major at Brown and found myself absolutely captivated by the history and magic of a wood stick. When I became friendly with David White, a Mohawk Indian who was the best player on our freshmen team, it seemed as if my life had found a new purpose. Whenever possible, I visited with Dave and his family at their home on the St Regis reservation in Hogansburg, NY. I could still only barely play the game when Dave got me in to some box games under the alias of "Ralph Cree." The standing joke was people on the reserve calling me "Ralph." Our house in the Adirondacks is decorated with the paintings of Dave's older daughter Joni and the younger one, Jade, was our team's manager during her undergraduate days here at UVA.

When I was asked in 1999 to join in an effort to create an annual award to honor the best men's and women's college lacrosse player, I was especially pleased to find the award's creators so determined to respect the game's Native American heritage. They went to the Iroquois elders to ask permission to simply even use the word Tewaaraton. I had little to do but remain very proud of the journey and the recognition that has accompanied the Tewaaraton Award history.

I come to the lacrosse community today with two things in mind. I believe we have an obligation to support our native brothers and sisters when they identify issues that have a serious negative impact on their communities. We have borrowed their Creator's game and it is time for us to begin to pay back that debt. When the Thompsons travel all the way to North Dakota to protest the pipeline, they should know that they travel with the support of all of us who were graced by their play. It is understandable that everyone may not be able to duplicate Scott Marr's remarkable dedication but we can always gather and provide financial, emotional and moral support (donate at ocetisakowincamp.org).

I also think we might take a page from the Tewaaraton Award founders' playbook. Let's shout out our history as America's oldest sport and our ties to the Native American community. We are always looking to grow the game while finding ourselves in an ever-increasingly competitive sports market. I believe if we identify and embrace the relationship to this land's noble indigenous roots, we distinguish ourselves in a homogenized market. A Native American presence at the NCAA Tournament and the accompanying telecasts, uniform helmet stickers, making it part of the IMLCA Hall of Fame, etc…let's grow the game, break that tired suburban stereotype and support a number of good causes. If the Creator chose to look down on us and blessed our efforts, we might make a real difference in people's lives.

Sincerely,

Dom Starsia
Head Coach Brown/UVA '83-'16

# 8

## The Pearly Gates

"St Peter, hey…how ya' doing? I am a little surprised to be here, certainly sooner than I expected but I had a pretty good run and I don't mind moving into your neighborhood. What's that, you need me to do one more thing? The Big Guy wants me to pick an alltime team from 1971, my first year in the game, till now, almost fifty years in the game, only ten players, chosen as if we had a game to play tonight. Not an easy task but, given my infinite alternative, I will give it my best shot."

"Getting ready to play a game" is a subtle shift from simply picking the best players at each position. On the attack, we need some balance and will look for two rights and a left. The rights will come from a group of five that includes, chronologically, Cornell's Eamon McEnaney, Casey Powell, Rob Pannell, Lyle Thompson and Pat Spencer. Eamon was a ferocious competitor, an All-Ivy wide receiver whose only loss in his three varsity seasons in Ithaca was in the '78 Finals versus Hopkins as a senior. Casey might simply be the very best lacrosse player I have seen live in my lifetime and may have made this group in two positions. I do not need to elaborate as much on the exquisite skills of Lyle and Rob who can still be seen in the pro ranks, nor Pat "I know I am jumping the gun here but this is how much respect

I have for this young man" Spencer. It should go without saying that these five were/are equally dangerous getting their own or elevating the play of those around them.

To play with two of these attackmen, we will need a lefty, more the consummate sniper, than someone who can carry and create. I might reach back to North Carolina State and suggest Stan Cockerton, whose scoring records stood until only recently. Maryland's Joe Walters, Duke's Zach Greer or Denver's Mark Matthews would be a better fit on this unit than the recently retired John Grant, Jr, Army's powerful Tom Cafaro or Brown's passing wizard Darren Lowe. Instead, I am going to go in a different direction here and choose Gary Gait as my third attackman. For two reasons, there was nothing Gary could not do on a lacrosse field. If Syracuse had needed him on the attack, he might have been the best that ever played. I have no doubt that he would have been a great fit with my other two attackmen—Eamon McEnaney and Casey Powell. That is my attack unit:

> Eamon McEnaney—Cornell '78
> Casey Powell—Syracuse '98
> Gary Gait—Syracuse '90

The second reason for choosing Gary as an attackman is that I could not leave one of my three middies off the team. There are some terrific middies to consider and a second line that included some combination of Hofstra's Vin Sombrotto, Syracuse's Brad Kotz or the Hopkins' duo of John Krumenacker and Del Dressel would be ridiculous. However, I can only take three (unlike the AA list these days that starts with a minimum of four) and the combination of athleticism and skill is unmistakable in my midfield unit of:

Frank Urso—Maryland '76
Jon Reese—Yale '90
Jay Jalbert—Virginia '00

Legend had it that Frank could have played football at Maryland and he intimidated opponents just walking out onto the field. Jon was an All-Ivy FB LB at Yale, made it to NFL camps and scored 80 (!!!) goals as a senior. Jay was the D1 Midfielder of the Year in his first college season playing the position, was an MLL and NLL All-Star and I believe he could have been an AA at any position on the field.

On defense, I realize that Dave Pietramala is the obvious choice. However, I am picking the team and I wasn't really paying attention to Hopkins during my years as the head coach at Brown. College coaches can be blind if they haven't seen someone up close as an opponent or consistent rival. I did not see a lot of Dave but he is going on to the team. To play alongside him, I could choose Maryland's Mike Thearle, who could almost break an attackman in half, Hopkins' John DeTomasso and Brian Voelker, Princeton's David Morrow or any number of those North Carolina defensemen from the '80s (Haus, Haus, Breschi, Cox). However, my final pair include an old school checker, Syracuse's Pat McCabe, who was more athletic than he appeared and could pick your pocket before you knew what happened. The final choice is actually the best defenseman I have seen in all my years, Georgetown's Brodie Merrill. He could cover any attackman, pick it off, pick it up and literally take away half the field. I first saw him playing box in

Canada after his commitment to Georgetown and walked away from the game thinking "I missed one there." My defense unit:

> Pat McCabe—Syracuse '91
> Dave Pietramala—Hopkins '89
> Brodie Merrill—Georgetown '05

My choice in the goal is someone that I did see way too much of during his college years. I did also see a lot of Cornell's Paul Schimoler up close and enough of Hopkins' Larry Quinn to appreciate their influence on a game. However, we got beat like a drum all four years that Sal Locasio was at UMass. He was also the New England Player of the Year all four years and those magic hands made the goal, at times, seem impenetrable. My goalie:

> Sal Locasio—UMass '89

Well, that's it...what do you say St Pete? I know there will be some controversy here but I will take my group and like my chances. Tell you what, I will let you coach this group if you punch this ticket!

# 9

## Dear Acacia

---

*The Boston College women's team lost a close game to the University of Maryland in the 2019 NCAA National Championship Game. It was their third consecutive appearance in the finals. I wrote this almost immediately following the game to their head coach Acacia Walker-Weinstein.*

Dear Acacia,

I thoroughly enjoyed meeting you for the first time at last year's Tewaaraton Ceremony. I had asked a mutual friend to introduce us. After watching your one-goal loss to James Madison just a few days prior, I wanted to simply provide you with someone who could commiserate with a couple of tough NCAA final game losses. In three of my first four years at Virginia we reached the semifinals and played through to OT of the final game in both '94 and '96. Coaches are always looking to improve, to "build a better mousetrap" but I also wanted to reassure you that your program had discovered the road to success and that drastic changes were probably not needed. Do what you are doing, keep getting back to that setting and the door may likely open when you least expect it.

I was thoroughly surprised when the Tufts men won their first NCAA Championship in 2010. Throughout my 22 years in

New England, I had never considered for a moment that Tufts was a "lacrosse school" and I had never met nor spoken with their coach, Mike Daley. I thought that the 2010 result may have been a blip on the screen and it was the next year when Tufts returned to the final game (to lose to Salisbury) that I called Daley the very next morning. I introduced myself and proceeded to say, "Mike, just want to congratulate you for this 2011 season, it is especially challenging to return to the final game."

Your team has now been to Championship Weekend each of these past three years and to the finals in each of those years. I read somewhere that consistency is the trademark characteristic of toughness and your program has demonstrated it in spades. It may take someone who has been in the heat of that moment to fully appreciate that the difference in the play of these two teams in a close-fought Championship Game is simply a whisper, a puff of smoke. In turn, the differences in the feeling for the two teams afterwards is monumental and so disproportionate to the differences in the play.

I am sure you love an incredible class of seniors. They carried themselves with class and dignity, provided leadership and a joy for all of us fans to watch. I am going to guess that there was a touch of extra pressure on them throughout the season. Our streak of three years was also led by a special class (two of whom are now in the US Lacrosse Hall of Fame...as a couple of yours will be one day) who had been to three Final Fours and two Final Games going into their senior year. From the outside, you would have envied the talent and experience we had going into that 1997 season. From within, I knew how badly they wanted to win that final game and how badly we wanted it for them. Much like your Eagles, we were a colorful, high flying group but that '97 season came with its severe expectations and maintained a challenging edge throughout.

Congratulations to Cathy Reese and the Terps on their National Championship and every bit to you and your team on a magnificent Final Weekend and a spectacular 2019 season. To your seniors, thank you for elevating the women's game on a national stage, for establishing a standard for effort and performance and...congrats on a great career. You have earned a proper celebration!

Sincerely,
Dom

# 10

## End of the Season Letter to Cannon's Players

8/18

Fellas, hey…born and raised in the NYC area, I have been a Yankees and NY Giants fan since about forever and you can feel free to consider that bias. When I think back to the 2007-8 NFL season, most fans dwell on the Giants beating the undefeated Patriots in the Super Bowl. While I was happy to see the Giants win that final game, I remain more in awe of the Giants performance in the final game of that regular season against a Patriots team that was highly motivated to finish undefeated going into the playoffs. The Giants had nothing to gain by getting after the Patriots that day, the final result would have no bearing on their playoff positioning. No one would have questioned resting their starters a week before their first round playoff match-up (as a wild card team, they were going on the road for every round). The 38-35 Patriots win was one of the most exciting games of that entire regular season. While never truly considering for a moment that the Giants would ever even reach the Super Bowl, never mind actually beat the Patriots…I do remember distinctly being a proud fan of a team that got after the undefeated Pats with nothing to really gain. When the Giants went on to win that Super Bowl, it was clear to me that they had set the table a month earlier by the quality of their effort in that "meaningless" final regular season game.

To make a long story longer, I thought about that whole Super Bowl episode at the end of this most recent Cannon's season. I don't like the expression "nothing to lose" (you work hard, everyone sacrifices...you always have something to play for) but we played our best lacrosse of the season after having been eliminated from playoff consideration. It's no small matter, I think most lacrosse "experts" would have predicted a different level of performance. We can be proud of the team's leadership on and off the field and of the steady progress we made throughout the year and of our performance at the end.

Now the real challenge begins...having raised our own expectations, we will certainly have our work cut out for us going forward. I believe we have a really strong nucleus of young talent on the team...now, we have to improve ourselves. If you did not dress enough to suit your own expectations, if you were on the edge of the line-up throughout the season and/or if you dressed and contributed in almost every game, you can significantly improve your own standing and performance during these next six months. You will look back at your time in the MLL and consider it as a comet in your life, it will come and go before you know it. What I am suggesting is that we really prepare to get after it in this next 2019 season. It will require a significant sacrifice to make this happen...everyone adjusts, personal, work, family...but, as long as I have been doing this, I can remind you that it is worth it. As good as we may have felt after the last game, the heavy lifting required in a championship effort creates a lifetime memory. Don't wait till tomorrow, start today.

Thanks for your welcoming spirit in my first MLL season, hope our paths cross again shortly, enjoy the remainder of the summer and stay in touch.

Dom

# LEADERSHIP

# 11

## Coaching Leadership

---

D o you want to know the single characteristic that distinguished every championship team in my coaching
lifetime? I thought you might. The answer is outstanding leadership. It can take some different forms and does not have to
be associated only with championship trophies but I have never
had a great team that did not have it in some abundance and
variation.

In turn, there are two distinct pieces to this athletic puzzle:
peer leadership among the players and coaching/administrative
leadership that creates the environment that nurtures the development of those qualities. We will address this latter category that
builds the foundation and supports the sustainability of a championship culture. In professional sports, it is more likely to be the
athlete, Tom Brady, Michael Jordan, Wayne Gretzky, etc. who
determines and distinguishes their team's achievements. From
youth sports through college, it is primarily the coaches who
define the most successful programs. Whether it is Mike Messere,
Anson Dorrance, Pat Summit, Cathy Reese, Jim Berkman or
Nick Saban, etc., it is the coaches who first come to mind. It
would be hard to overstate the measure of their influence over the
young men and women at their respective institutions. What are

the characteristics and requirements for coaching leadership in a successful lacrosse program?

*Men (and women) of value have scars* …Michael Jordan was cut from his high school basketball team, Brady largely ignored in the draft, Belichek fired from his position as head coach of the Cleveland Browns. The Maryland men's team could not have endured much more than the 42 years and 9 title games that passed between National Championships. Someone saw something in those men and we all respected the passion and determination of the Terps during their championship drought.

I have a few of those scars and how any one of us deals with them will likely have as much to do with the person we will become as any of the championships and awards. An ability to persevere and to grow may be the first component as relates to our topic of leadership. It is about having lived a real and genuine life with the pain and joy that are part of the package. When people know you have suffered some, it helps to get their attention, to have them feel as if they can better relate to the message and the messenger. The pain in your life, the failures, can be profound teaching tools. A common theme for me will be opening up to the people around you, to those you want to lead. Whatever your message, it will gather strength when woven with real life experiences.

*Do your own laundry*…my wife says I am making this up, but for me it is a vivid memory. When we first were living together, I was standing there holding my dirty laundry and innocently asked, "what do you want me to do with this?" Her reply was a cleaned-up version of "I don't give a hoot what you do with it." Truth is, I have done my own laundry these past 40 years. You need to be willing to serve before you can lead.

What I am suggesting is that leaders "walk the walk." I would never ask someone to do something I was not willing to do myself. Whether it is picking up balls, carrying a bag, opening a door, etc., there is no job I would have asked a player, an assistant, the strength coach, the janitor to do that I would not have simply done myself. Things that need to be done are never "beneath" me, they rest alongside scoring goals, making saves and all the other things that go into creating a winning environment. It was always gratifying to me at the end of a practice when we were searching for balls to see the seniors and All-Americans two fields over while the freshmen were gathered together in the middle of the field comparing their high school exploits. The older guys got the message.

*You can never take it back*...I became a better, more successful, coach when I learned to talk to my staff and players in a positive way. Coaches are often the smartest and most clever people on a practice field and the players give us lots of material for biting sarcasm. I know how hard it can be to bite your tongue but you will win more, be more successful if you can make this adjustment in your language. Working to encourage loyalty in the people around us is to speak with them respectfully. They never forget.

*People hearing without listening*...that iconic lyric of Paul Simon reminds us that being a good listener is a powerful skill for a confident leader. The people we are trying to reach need to know that we are open to their commentary, empathetic to their needs and willing to make adjustments. At the same time, there are limits to the amount of input, especially from a group. Too many opinions can limit efficiency, create confusion, and is almost inversely proportional to constructive consensus. Be a good listener, for a while. You are going to have to make the final call anyway, know when to cut to the chase.

*Take responsibility...*The best teacher I had as an undergraduate at Brown was in Education. He consistently emphasized that a teacher is responsible for EVERYTHING that goes on in their classroom...students not paying attention, students being unruly, etc...everything fell on the shoulders of the teacher. It was a message that really hit home. You're an educator, a teacher, a coach, the players are your students, the weight room, the locker room, the practice field, your classroom. "We're not getting better, they're not listening to me, we're not improving, etc."...don't blame them, don't blame others, figure it out, fix it, create an environment where they are learning, where they are engaged, where they get a chance to grow. You don't get to pass the blame, you don't get to take a day off...leaders are always on and always step up when hard things are being decided.

*Strengthen your team from the bottom up...* One of the most important tasks of those in a leadership role is to convince each and every person in the chain of command of how important each of their roles will be in determining our ultimate success. I would be so bold to tell you that I became absolutely convinced over the course of a long career that everyone's role was equally important. Different?, yes, of course, but equally important. While one person, almost anyone on a team or in an organization, can lift the entire group, the inverse is also true, one person can bring it all down. We are only as strong as our weakest link...make the least important feel as if he is the most. When the last guy on the roster is first in the running, it forces the guys who get all the attention on game day to elevate their effort and performance.

*Make it personal...*I often use a variation of this expression in reference to the recruiting. It also applies in this context...to be an effective leader, you need good people around you. In fact, the most important factor in this entire exercise may be an emphasis on finding good people and keeping them on board. A sports psychologist might have a field day but I always felt that I was too busy to try and separate work and family. I talked with my players the way I spoke with my children and the values that mattered at home were carried into the locker room. What is the difference between Carolina and Virginia, Penn and Brown, Lehigh and Colgate, etc? Generally, it is us. You need good people, you want to keep good people...make it about you and your family, make it about their family, don't be afraid to show people some vulnerability, show them you care.

*Authenticity is a scent,* and so is a lack of authenticity...I may not quite be sure how to define this quality but, I sure as heck can tell when it enters the room. Authenticity is about honesty and is some combination of walking the walk and making it personal. It is hard to say something meaningful to a team every day. On those days, rather than making up some false narrative, I will often open by simply saying "I can't think of anything clever to say today." I can't tell you how satisfying it is to look at their faces and have their expressions calmly replying in an unspoken way, "no sweat coach, we've got your back." One of my favorites is telling them that my motivating them the day before a game is like getting ready for that first date. Man, you just want to say the right thing to have this girl think you are just the coolest. We all know that impression fades quickly. What prevails in the end is the substance of your character, your preparation. That is what will truly make the difference. When your team is woven into the fabric of your life, when the people around you know you would do anything for them and they would do anything for you, that is the picture of effective leadership.

*It's worth it...*if you asked me to boil down into one sentence what it is that I have been doing these past 42 years, it has been trying to convince young men that it is worth the sacrifices that are required in order to be successful. If leadership is defined as an individual's ability to influence others, hardly an hour has gone by in my life when I was not considering how to make that point more effectively. But, that's it...gathering good people and convincing them that it is worth the sacrifices, whatever it is we are asking them to do. Don't be afraid to tell them that it is hard, it's supposed to be hard, hard reminds us that the endeavor is special. In fact, if it doesn't feel hard, tell them that they are not working hard enough at it. At the same time, don't forget to tell them there is hardly anything more worthwhile than what can be attained by accomplishing something as a group.

One last thought...it is how you treat people that will ultimately define the measure of your ability to lead them.

*"The essence of leadership is vision. You can't blow an uncertain trumpet."*

Father Theodore Hesburgh

# 12

# Leadership Qualities for the Players

The next chapter in our examination of the qualities of exceptional leadership lies in the area that directly affects our athletes. How do they influence one another? This is a more visceral canvass than the administrative component that involves the coaches. As we consider the development of leadership skills among players, what role does the question of nurture v. nature play? Are we born with a predisposition toward the qualities which distinguish outstanding leadership? Can they be taught? Is there a role for the concept of "10,000 hours" in the development of those qualities?

While I might prefer the dramatic announcement of some profound revelation or scientific breakthrough, as with most questions of this nature, the truth probably lies somewhere closer to the middle. The smoothest two-handed stickwork I have ever witnessed belonged to either Jeff Long or Steele Stanwick. I have heard all the stories of Steele, the wall in that garage on University Ave. and all the hours he put in pounding the ball. On the other hand, I could be banging the ball off that same wall till my hands bled and I would never develop that unconscious offhand. I am convinced that for both Jeff and Steele, at least some of that magical suppleness is a genetic gift. I believe our culture does a good job of identifying young people with special physical skills and channeling them in a well-suited direction.

However, it has become increasingly more difficult to identify and encourage in young people the subtle skills that will mature and blossom into exceptional leadership. I always dreamed I would someday be the starting shortstop for the NY Yankees but long before I came to terms with my severe limitations, I was the one organizing the teams and picking the sides. Consider the last time you were aware of young people going to the field to "choose up." Youth sports are so adult-organized these days, where/how would a young athlete begin to develop leadership skills? I will come back to the requirement of fearlessness as a component of effective peer leadership but how do kids develop that skill when parents and our modern culture seem so intent on removing all the risk from our upbringing—risk of injury, risk of failure, risk of risk, etc? Having been around young people most of my adult life, the biggest change over 42 years may be an institutional reluctance to allow these same young participants to figure things out on their own. The world needs more real leaders but they are making the developmental process much more difficult to engineer.

While I have always felt strongly that you cannot impose leadership from the top down, under the right, spontaneous circumstance, it can bubble up from below and carry a willing partner to transcendent heights. When UVA won the National Championship in 2011, we were not nearly as talented a team as many that had come before. Midway through the season we lost our best defenseman to injury, dismissed our two most talented players and took two hard, consecutive conference losses. It was a season about to spiral out of control. In the midst of those circumstances, a young man who simply refused to be discouraged,

Steele Stanwick being honored at halftime in 2013, waving to Maggie and Emma

Bray Malphrus with Maggie and Emma, May, 2011

walked into my office and calmly notified me "I know that was hard for you (the dismissals), we are ready to go." Bray Malphrus was not always a great leader in our program. Earlier in his career he was more interested in his own interpretation of the universe. By his senior year, however, he became much more invested in the welfare of the people around him, and, of the team. He had not always been a great leader but, he became one. His transformation provides an encouraging and inspired lesson and you are likely not surprised to hear that he became a decorated Army Ranger.

I have mentioned fearlessness as one of the primary characteristics of exceptional leadership. It is more about fearlessness, rather than confidence. Fearlessness is more of an instinct, confidence can be an acquired taste. It often comes later or reluctantly to someone who lives/competes/succeeds in a challenging environment. But, fearlessness is that little kid who ran right into the tree chasing that pop up, the one to whom it would simply never occur not to take the open shot with the game on the line, the one whose body language is always exclaiming "watch me, this is how we roll" and who was willing to "choose up the teams." Fearlessness stands up in front of the team and sets an uncompromising agenda and then, walks into the coach's office with the same conviction. Fearlessness takes his standards to the edge of unreasonableness but, without going over the line.

The second characteristic of exceptional leadership is selflessness. This is explicitly not about being unselfish. All great athletes are competitively selfish. They want the ball, they unintentionally crave the dramatic, deciding moment and we applaud this instinct but, the leaders are unyielding about their own role with regards to the welfare of the team. They consistently demonstrate a willingness to do whatever it takes in order to create the conditions for success. Tim Whiteley, VA '96, never hesitated to play primarily in his offhand to facilitate an attack unit generally recognized as one of the game's best ever and led Virginia to three consecutive semifinal appearances. Tim's selflessness may have been the team's lynchpin for success and come at the cost of his legacy alongside his two Hall of Fame line mates.

True leaders are honest. I have always encouraged athletes to be supportive of their teammates, to talk with them in a positive tone. You can still accomplish this while telling your teammates the truth. It may still be a bitter pill to hand a peer but teammates learn to trust and coaches come to respect those unwilling to compromise in this area. I might even advocate to those who aspire to be a team's leader that if you cannot tell your teammates the truth, don't accept a captaincy role. Your equivocation will invariably complicate too many organizational relationships. I was once asked about the common characteristics of teams that did not begin to reach their playing potential and my reply was that there was a lack of trust among the participants on those teams. I would suggest to coaches that a core value of any team should be the creation of an atmosphere of honesty throughout the program.

It is almost a requirement that your exceptional leaders are among the team's very hardest workers. The inverse is clearly not necessarily the case but you cannot expect to lead if you don't set the tone. The old adage that you especially like your chances if your hardest worker is also your best player is very true. A leader does not actually have to finish first in every exercise but his effort does. Chris Rotelli won the Tewaaraton Award and led Virginia to the 2003 National Championship in the mud at Ravens Stadium. He may have actually won every run, at every distance, from September to May, in his senior year. He scored fewer goals in 2003 than in each of the previous two years but he became a leader and a champion.

Self-discipline is a critical component for anyone who expects to lead. I believe you want to be with your teammates away from the field and locker room. However, you need to be a consistent voice of reason and cannot fall prey to serious substance abuse violations. You forfeit any sense of moral authority in an area of vital importance to the development of a college team.

I am going to combine the final two categories because I see them as closely related. First and foremost, leaders need to "walk the walk," they need to follow-through on what they are asking of their teammates, they need to be at the front of the line when the work is being done and they need to be the ones who take the risks on and off the field. They need to be tough, with a tenacity and relentlessness of spirit. In my playing lifetime, that is who I always tried to be and I always thought that was enough. It is not. I was raised that your actions spoke louder than your words. There is, however, another requirement of athletic leadership that now speaks directly to an emerging interpretation of toughness. You can be the strong silent type and you can be really tough and you can be a great player, but you cannot be an exceptional leader unless you are also a willing and compelling communicator. Jay Bilas in his book "Toughness" talks about the toughness required to be a communicator on the basketball court. It is related to an unwavering personal commitment to place your teammate's and the team's welfare above your comfort level. It is a constant reminder to your teammates that you will be there for them in every circumstance, on and off the field. To be a truly effective leader, the right words need to be said.

If I was speaking to a group of young people and we were forging a blueprint for the rest of their entire athletic life, I would suggest that the overriding goal would be to develop into someone considered an exceptional leader by their peers. You could not get to that place without expanding your physical capabilities to their near limit. The journey will take you to all your other goals.

To become that leader in a team sport setting, you will need a streak of fearlessness, a selfless consideration for your team and teammates, you need to be able to speak the truth to your peers, you need to be one of your program's hardest workers, radiate self-discipline, be tough and engaged at all times. We stand in awe when examples of this behavior distinguish themselves in an athletic setting. Even more importantly, our world needs more true leaders.

Thank you

# 13

## How Do We Teach Leadership?

When I began my coaching career in the fall of 1974, the first adjustment was the unexpected challenge of learning to articulate the things that I had always been able to do instinctively as a player. How did I anticipate a play unfolding? Why was I able to find the open man in the clearing game?, etc. It took considerable time for me to figure out what I had been doing in order to teach it to others. As I have thought about this topic of leadership (and others), I find myself going through a similar exercise. I have been blessed throughout my career with some outstanding captain/leaders. Without any conspicuous intention, I believe we created an environment for these individuals to flourish. The "how did that happen and how can I explain it" will be the aim of this composition.

I have heard Eric Kapitulik, a former Navy Seal and director of The Program, answer the question of "how many captains should you have on a team?" with an emphatic "one!" His strong belief is that there can only be one uninterrupted voice on a squadron/team. I have disagreed respectfully but openly; there are too many peripheral issues with college students to drop all that responsibility on one person. In the military, it is "life and death," the mission is clear, there can be no equivocation in the group response, people might die. In college, there are all kinds of incidental matters involved in putting a team together…study hall attendance, academic performance, locker room culture, administrative responsibilities, behavior off the field, effort on the field, etc. Here is the way I see it now…you can have and might need multiple captains (and that can vary by situation) but there is only one true leader. As I have looked back on all the teams in my career, when we have that one person standing up above all the others, we have a chance for something special.

I was on the phone with Mike Murphy, head coach at UPenn, recently and we were discussing all the variables that interact with the development of leadership for college students. He felt strongly that the most important piece of information that he needed was the "how to" in teaching leadership skills to his players. I was immediately tempted to google it, I was sure there were countless books on the subject, the academies designated an entire curriculum just to this topic. I have decided to leave all those options to you. For the purposes of this essay, we are going to go with one man's gut instinct and the first-hand experience of having survived 42 years of working with college lacrosse players. This will be my personal interpretation of a profoundly important issue for coaches.

First and foremost, a coach needs to be a role model for his players. We talked about those qualities earlier, and I would suggest that this is the most important responsibility for someone who aspires to lead and influence others.

You need to identify the players who begin to demonstrate the qualities of leadership. I would begin that process early in a young man's career. Sometimes it is obvious when they simply walk through the door: more often than not, however, there are telltale signs early that still need to be developed. The same way that we assess and work with players on different skills/

strengths, we identify those with leadership potential and devise a plan to nurture those attributes. What are we looking for? Is someone a hard worker? Does he steadily improve throughout the year (in the weight room, conditioning tests, is he steady in the classroom?, etc.)? Does he demonstrate a resilient spirit? Do his teammates respond to him in a positive way? Is his competitiveness and tenacity in practice respected by his teammates? Is there an early, spontaneous example of him standing up to his teammates (does not have to be a big, dramatic circumstance early on)?

I go back and forth a little on this next one but, I don't think you need to tell such player(s) early on what your long-range intention (leadership development) is here. Some may not progress in this area and drift away and I believe there is real merit to others thinking they figured these things out for themselves. The roots are deeper when there are some spontaneous developments/demonstrations of leadership. You will also find that the results will be more profound.

You need to cultivate a program of openness and honesty. Encourage these selected players to come in your office individually or in small groups to talk with you and with each other. Keep the meetings on a regular schedule, first Monday of each month, i.e., well-intentioned ideas often get away from us. You don't need a hard agenda but having some topics in mind will keep things moving. Let them know that everything is on the table. Make the conversations personal and meaningful. You can talk about the circumstances that define leadership. Send them relevant articles about examples of leadership, suggest books to read. Are they intrigued by the information? Do they follow up?

The players need to know they can come in and talk with you. They may be clumsy, the meetings a little awkward at first... no worries, they are finding their way, their leadership "sea legs."

It is simply human nature for it to take a while before you are both comfortable getting to know each other, and our own unease and adaptation to each individual is part of the fascination in our profession. Telling someone that you do not know all the answers is an intimate way to gain their trust. If they come to appreciate the complex organization of a team and the myriad challenges facing coaches, they will be more likely to stand up for you in moments of stress.

In the previous chapter, I had talked about the roles that Bray Malphrus and Chris Rotelli had played on championship teams in 2011 and 2003. In Bray's case, early in his career, he wanted black and white answers to every situation that came up at the defensive end of the field. I could sense his frustration when I would tell him that it simply does not work that way. He did not want to hear that "this is a fluid game, you are going to have to react and figure it out on the fly." In turn, I think Chris was startled when my reaction to his being selected first team All-ACC in 2001 was "you have so much more to offer us." He may have been disappointed at my lack of effusive praise for his 35 point All-Conference performance. In both their cases, we talked for years before they fully put the team and their teammates performances before their own. They weren't selfish or immature, in fact just the opposite, but their eyes opened to the vast possibilities of their own roles. Bray led the lowest ranked team with the most losses to an unlikely NCAA Championship and while Chris scored fewer goals than in his soph season, his 25 goal/25 assist senior performance was the first by a middie in ACC history (Chris was also the first lacrosse player to be selected the ACC Male Athlete of the Year). Both those teams had other excellent captains/leaders but it was Bray and Chris who singularly stood out.

Following a subpar exhibition performance in the fall of 1998, our staff decided to make every remaining activity till the end of the semester a competitive exercise. We divided the team up, assigned captains, kept score and standings and played for an overall, informal championship. Weight room work, conditioning runs, basketball and soccer games and touch football that almost required equipment. We created an environment for our leaders to assume responsibility, to interact and impact their teammates. I am hesitant to draw a straight line from process to result but we captured Virginia's first national championship in 27 years that spring.

It is important for a team to recognize that the final responsibility for disciplinary action lies with the head coach. It makes for an unequivocal signal to the offending player, his teammates, parents, administrators, etc., that the head coach makes the final call. You do not want players blaming each other or assistant coaches even in situations that clearly require some punishment. However, getting the team leaders involved in a discussion of the situation and considerations will be a gesture of trust and respect. How would they handle this particular situation? It will also help them to understand that there are larger issues at play than their own comfort level or that of a teammate. They will begin to acknowledge their own status in the program and that the coach has confidence in their ability to handle some tight spots.

You have identified the 2-3 players in your program who may have these special qualities...now, identify people in your community, your institution, alums, former players, etc. who you KNOW have these qualities. Call this latter group, maybe out of the blue, and arrange to have them meet with one of these players one on one. I do not think you will have any trouble getting them to agree, true leaders want to share. You are hoping that the meeting creates a synergy, a spark, that they will unwittingly speak a language to each other that is not unlike a dog whistle, that they will say things to each other that the rest of us cannot hear.

Finally, look for an extended period of time when the team could be involved in meaningful activities that do not include the coaches. Whether it is a break in the middle of the off season or, perhaps, the last week of the fall semester, designate it as "captains' week." No specific planning by the coaches, no sneak peeks, etc., let the captains/leaders run the show. Afterwards, you can sit and talk about what it was like, what they might have done differently, what were the headaches. Whatever they may be missing from the guidance of coaches may be made up for in an increased sense of initiative and responsibility.

I have been thinking about this subject for some time now but it occurs to me that I never consciously thought to teach leadership. I was raised and educated in an environment that advocated for personal responsibility and individual initiative. It was an unintentional coaching priority to create an atmosphere for the blossoming of leadership and I was blessed to have a number of young men step into these roles. I can acknowledge now that it is a learned skill that needs to be identified and nurtured. Be patient, be open, firm and fair. The young man with those genuine leadership roots may be ready to emerge at the critically decisive moment and have the most profound influence on those around him.

I will leave you with an affirming quote from Vince Lombardi... "Leaders aren't born, they are made. And they are made just like everything else, through hard work. And that's the price we'll have to pay to achieve that goal, or any goal."

Good luck!

# 14

# The Language of Leadership

In our previous articles on leadership, I had talked about the language of coaches and the lasting effect our comments can have on athletes. The young people in our charge are much more likely to respond in a productive manner to consistently mindful and positive dialogue. In fact, I felt one of the primary responsibilities of a coach was to say something meaningful every day. One of the great joys of this profession is to have a former athlete repeat something you said at an earlier moment as an example of a lesson in his/her life.

It has recently occurred to me that the flip side of this principle is also true. I have had athletes say things to me that have had a profound effect on my coaching and in my own life. In most instances it was not a calculated statement, more a spontaneous reaction, a truthful expression. I would describe this as athletes using the "language of leadership." I always tell young players to aspire to be a leader, that the journey to true leadership will take you to all your individual playing goals. We may recognize a leader when we see him/her but what does it sound like? Genuine leadership speaks in the first-person. It is not simply "let's go" to your teammates, it is much more

Undefeated Brown 1991 Seniors

often in word and action "watch me." Some people are not as good with the words, and your actions at the consistently critical moments speak volumes. However, there are also moments when the right words clarify the message and serve a necessary purpose. To these same young athletes, I would suggest this...close your eyes and try to imagine some variation of these words coming out of your own mouth as you consider the evolution of your athletic career.

In 1991, our Brown team was 6 & 0, about to play Yale, NCAA semifinalist from the year before and our first Ivy opponent, on a Wednesday in Providence. We were coming off a bye weekend and the players were required back in town for a community service project on Sunday afternoon. Andy Towers, a 1st team AA middie, our FO man and perhaps our best player, missed his ride and the Sunday activity. He called along the way to apologize and I told him not to come to Monday's practice.

A couple of the older players came to speak to me afterwards. They were making the case for needing him for Wednesday's game. I slept on it and told everyone he had to sit for the game, there are consequences for actions and decisions. When Andy asked to speak to the team after Tuesday's practice, I had some concerns but said OK. He stepped into the team huddle and said "Dom is right, I made a mistake, I deserve to sit, you will beat Yale tomorrow without me." We did beat Yale and Andy was one of the finest game day managers I have ever had. The episode galvanized the team and we finished the regular season 13 & 0.

In 1992, my final spring at Brown, we got beat 17-12 by Loyola in the first round of the Fleet Tournament. We were playing an NCAA-bound Duke team the next day and were still licking our wounds at a team meeting that evening. I was concerned about the mood of the team until future Hall of Famer Darren Lowe had the last word of the day: "if you want to know how this will go tomorrow, watch me." Darren was 3 & 7 and we beat Duke 16-4.

My second season at UVA was the spring of 1994. There was some selfishness in the locker room and our season was spiraling downward, especially after getting beaten by UNC in the finals of the ACC Tournament 15-7. It was hard not to be discouraged until two freshmen, Doug Knight and Brian Birch, walked in my office and declared, "enough of that, we will not lose again." Now, neither was a starter but their laser focus became a contagion for the entire team. We went on to beat a higher ranked UNC team on the road in the NCAA quarterfinals, the #1 seed Syracuse in 2 OT's after being down five and two men down to start the fourth quarter in the semis and came back from three down in the 4th quarter to force OT in the final against Princeton. While we lost that final game, our program turned a corner and took on a different edge.

I ran into junior defenseman Darren Mahoney late in the 1996 season. He had been inserted into the line-up midway through that season and had just been terrific down the stretch. I actually apologized to Darren for not getting him into the line-up earlier in his career and he responded "Coach, I'm sure it was just the right time for me to play." He was a captain and leader in 1997.

Eerily similar to 1994, we found ourselves down three in the fourth quarter again in 1996's NCAA Final. We came storming back and found ourselves in the huddle about to face-off in OT. We used two FO guys throughout the season and throughout the game and I was not certain who would take this important draw. UVA had not won a National Championship in 24 years when I glanced across the huddle and David Wren looked me in the eye and mouthed the words, "I got this one." I could not have asked for anything more from an athlete than that reaction in that setting. The fact that we did not win the FO nor the game speaks to the reality of life itself. We do not make every shot, we do not win every game but the willingness to step to the center of the battle at the critical moment defines our character.

We finally won our championship in 1999 and after all the anguish of 27 years, it was left to senior defenseman Courtland Weisleder to simply state "that wasn't so hard." So profound in its simplicity, I use it over and over again to explain to young people that it is the anticipation of the sacrifice and commitment that seems so overwhelming. If you happen to reach your goals, you can only barely imagine why the decision to take this journey seemed so daunting.

It was the summer of 2002 and we were looking to put two goalies in the incoming class. Our first choice was Bud Petit, the U-19 US Team member. We offered the second spot to Kip Turner and we were forthright about the situation. He was not especially pleased and asked to think about it through the weekend. When we spoke next, Kip said "I have one question, will I have a fair chance when I get there?" I assured him that he would have 40 teammates who would be certain that we played the best goalie. Kip sat behind Tillman Johnson for a year and then started the next three, including the 2006 undefeated national championship season. To his great credit, Bud did not make it into the line-up until his fifth year, when he carried the 2008 team to the national semifinals.

We struggled with issues on and off the field in 2004 and the common assumption would have been to crack down hard in 2005. Junior defenseman Mike Culver came in to talk following 2004 and surprised me with "Coach, you are going to have to trust us." When I assured him that the price for my trust would be more severe consequences for any transgressions, he was fully prepared to bear that responsibility. I do not recall a single issue during those two years and we played some of the finest lacrosse in the game's history.

Here is an example of the "unspoken language of leadership." It was the fall of 2008 and our returning attack included Danny Glading and Garrett Billings. We needed one of our talented incoming attackmen, Steele Stanwick and Chris Bocklet, to play on their off-lefthanded side in their first year. I mentioned that to both Steele and Chris early in the summer before their arrival...they could help the team and get on the field quicker, if they could manage on the left side. It was the first rep, of the first drill, of the first fall practice that saw Steele jump into the front of the lefthanded line for a 3 v 2 drill coming off the endline. I swear it may have been the first ball I ever saw him shoot, he dropped his hands and ripped it low to high in the upper corner. He sort of looked over at me and without saying a word, his body language screamed "I am going to take care of this for you." Steele scored close to 40 goals that year and I will bet that 35 were lefthanded.

Finally, there was one game to go in our 2011 regular season. Our record was 7 & 5, we had just been clobbered in consecutive games, our best defenseman was recovering from season-ending surgery and I had just dismissed two of our leading players from the team. I was concerned that we were closer to disarray than to the NCAA playoffs. It was two days from our final regular season game against an NCAA-bound Penn team when senior captain Bray Malphrus came to me to affirm "I know how hard that was for you Coach (the dismissals), we are ready to go." We went on to beat Penn and win the NCAA Championship with the most regular season losses in playoff history. Along with Steele and John Haldy, one of the great demonstrations of athletic leadership.

Here is one for the parents...usually you make a scholarship offer before a young man commits. When one of our top recruits committed before we made our offer, I went on to tell him "and, oh, by the way, here is what we have in mind for your partial scholarship." I received a text message later that evening from his mother who said she needed to talk with me the next day, uh oh...She called the next day to say, "Dom, we have been blessed, we don't need the scholarship, please give it to someone on the team who needs it more."

These are the memories that live on for me, these are the stories that I re-tell, that changed my life. The championships and the games have been breathtaking. At the same time, it is these very real moments that fill up your soul.

Andy Towers graduates from Brown, 1993

# 15

## Who Will Win in 2017?...Look to the Leaders

L et me put you at a place where I found myself a short time ago. After having spent almost two days with Andy Kay's MICDS team in St Louis this past March and immediately after having met with the players, a junior on the team, Alexander Feldman, came up to me and asked "what is the defining quality for outstanding leadership in your players?" How would you have responded in just that moment? There are a number of descriptive attributes that quickly come to mind...unselfishness, charisma, toughness, discipline, talent and certainly some combination of all these (and others) are included.

I took a deep breath, turned to Alex and said that "fearlessness" was my choice as the single defining quality of outstanding leadership. How many young men and women of college age are willing to stand up in front of their peers and assume a position of uncompromising responsibility to the common goal? They need to be willing to take that conviction to the absolute edge of unreasonableness without going over the line. "This is what we are doing, this is how we are doing it and nothing is going to interfere in our pursuit." I am telling you that one player, fully committed, can lift an entire team. If that player happens to be your best player, all the better but,

Tucker Radebaugh, Co-captain of our first National Champion Team 1999

that's not the requirement. At the same time, this person needs to be respected by the staff and willing to walk into the coach's office ready to speak up for his teammates. I am describing a special person.

In 1999, for the University of Virginia, that player was Tucker Radebaugh. When we talk about futility streaks in our sport, Virginia's 27 year absence from the championship podium had significant status alongside Maryland's 0 & 9 record in National Championship games since 1975 and marginalizes Virginia's recent struggles in the ACC and against Duke. Tucker had won the team's Leadership Award after both his soph and junior seasons (respect of the staff) and he was not the best player on the team. However, he made a personal decision going into the summer of 1998 and I can still see him from my office window, running up and down the hills adjacent to the practice field in the middle of July holding a 45 pound plate above his head. When the team assembled again in September, it was the beginning of a conversation that defined the sacrifices that would be required to break the 27 year hex. Tuck put pressure on the staff and his teammates but it was going to get done and, it did.

I have been blessed in my career to only have worked at two schools that may be more likely to produce young men of such singular caliber. I think it is more uncommon but possible that a group of young men on a team can work together to produce that laser focus of responsibility. Our 2006 undefeated National Championship team had a collective will of "nothing gets in the way of the lacrosse."

We seem to all agree that 2017 has been an unprecedented year in our sport. While I am not convinced that parity has actually arrived, I would be the first to admit that unpredictability is out in full force. What I would suggest to the playoff prognosticators is to spend a little less time looking for the hot goalie or the best face-off man and try to determine who has the high quality senior leaders. Can you determine which of these young men is inclined to stand up in front of his peers and "assume the position"? There are so many variables going on behind the scenes in a college locker room that it would be hard to make this determination from the outside looking in. However, when the postscript of 2017 is written, I will not be surprised if a group of one is not the difference for the winning team.

Tuck, May 1999

# 16

# "A Priest and a Rabbi Walk into a Bar..."

During this holiday season, approaching the new year and with the 2019 season on the near horizon, I would like to make a recommendation to coaches at all levels, one that combines an approach to our profession with a state of mind. While I was still coaching at Brown, the athletic department staff was required at an all-day professional development workshop. I did not mind getting out of the office but I was skeptical of learning any lessons that might truly impact my life/career. However, the message that day was how using positive language with your athletes would make you a better coach, a more successful coach. It wasn't about talking to your athletes in a positive manner once in a while, it was about framing your language in that tone all the time. It is the subtle difference between "don't foul" and "make the smart play." You are taking more of a chance by trusting your athletes to interpret the "smart play" but you are elevating your relationship with those same athletes in a critical moment. I have often been asked by coaches about the common thread that ran through our most successful teams. While we were hardly ever as talented as the fans and the players' parents thought we were, we were generally good enough to win. What distinguished those uncommon teams was their ability and willingness to trust themselves, each other and the staff. Every interaction with your athletes has a bearing on those relationships. Imagine the confidence your athletes will display if they truly feel that "he trusts me."

I have always felt that the things I have said to my athletes are the same that I would be using with my children at home. You either believe something to be true and have it apply in all situations or those we influence will sense your shading. Now, when the ball is rolling down the driveway toward the street with my six year old in full pursuit, I am much less interested in his "making the smart play" than I am in his "don't run in the street." For coaches and parents, these are the conversations we have on the practice field and in the yard. Recreating those end-of-the-game situations, talking through the variables and hoping/trusting that they will come to understand what constitutes the smart play. You may have to bite your tongue, it may take more time than you think you have and you may come up short in the near term. But, just as I learned, you will win more in the long run.

The second piece of this message is related to the first. I have been around so many men's and women's programs in these past two and a half years and have been so impressed with the quality of the young people in the coaching profession. I am not giving any one of you good news when I tell you that all your peers are working...hard, diligent in their pursuit of the keys to success. I tell athletes all the time that working hard is not enough, and the same goes for coaches. Concerning yourself with the certainty that you are watching more film than your peers, producing longer scouting reports, spending more time on the practice field, etc. would actually take time away from the fundamental development of an understanding of what coaches do for a living..."we are in a people business."

In just the two and a half years since I was last on a college sideline, the technological developments now at your disposal are stunning. I have seen drones on the practice field, multiple cameras that can focus on a single player throughout the practice, coaches using IPADS between repetitions, etc., all providing valuable information. I realize there is more at stake with each passing day as salaries have increased, conference championships in play, AD's paying more attention and with less patience than just a few years ago. My concern is that these same good, young, earnest coaches develop a countenance so serious that it is counterproductive to their actual intent.

I am confident that most of us have told our athletes on more than one occasion that being on the practice field or in the weight room or locker room is the best part of our day. Is that how you truly feel? If it is (and it likely is!), you need to radiate that joy to your athletes. You can't force it, players can smell inauthenticity but, if you have an easy, genuine smile, your players will take it as a cue that they can relax and enjoy the task. Players will learn better with a smile on their face, they will have an open mind. Players who smile are resilient of spirit and tend to be optimists. Isn't that what we want in our athletes?

Never mind making the conference tournament; with lives on the line, it was General Dwight David Eisenhower who said "A sense of humor is part of the art of leadership, of getting along with people, of getting things done." Having that joy in your heart, that smile on your face radiates professionalism and confidence to your athletes. I read somewhere that a sense of humor is an expression of goodness and wisdom together. That is the task you are charged with each and every day. With all the daily pressures, it is still simply convincing your players to love the moment.

Back to the "priest and the rabbi...," all this has nothing to do with jokes, not sure I ever told one in 42 years. It is not about having fun and it is certainly not about making it easier on your players. Athletes want to be pushed, they want to work hard, they want to test their limits. The balance here for coaches is to help their athletes understand that the discomfort that accompanies sweat, failure, repetition, resiliency and aspiration is what makes the athletic journey so meaningful. The short sighted among us get pre-occupied with grab-assing in the back of the line, gossiping with teammates between drills and/or those with the clipboard convincing themselves that more work and more yelling is a suitable substitute for an enlightened narration. It may have been Lord Byron who said "there is no joy the world can give like that which comes from joining good men in common purpose." That is what we are striving for on the practice field. When you see it manifest itself and feel it in your bones, don't stifle the smile that you and your players have earned. The oxymoron in me is trying to make your team tougher, more consistent by having you lighten up a little. It is about a sense of trust, of how you treat people and of being able to communicate (and for you to live it) about the importance of this balance in a person's life. Reach out to your athletes, check in daily with the one down at the end of the bench, don't be afraid to show some personal vulnerability. We teach young players not to squeeze the stick, I am trying to convince you not to squeeze the whistle.

# 17

# A True Teammate

You might need some history in the game but you would not need to be a highly-educated lacrosse fan to recognize that Cornell was the "Team of the Decade" in the 1970s. From a National Championship in the first NCAA-sanctioned tournament in 1971 to the end of a streak of three consecutive undefeated seasons in the Finals in 1978. It was an impressive run.

The Big Red were even more dominant in the Ivy League, capturing Ivy crowns in 15 of the 16 years between 1968 and 1983. They were undefeated in league play in the three years prior to arriving in Providence for a game against Brown in 1973. Bruce Arena was the captain and star of a heavy favorite who anticipated keeping that streak alive.

Brown was led by its Massapequa, NY, senior captain, attackman Stephan Russo. "Steph" was a different soul, especially so from the perspective of a stereotypical lacrosse jock. He barely wanted you to know he was an athlete, certainly did not want to be judged by those standards. He was a competitor, though, and an aggressive streak belied his off-the-field personality.

Steph was struggling some in the early stages of that '73 season. Recovering from a knee injury contributed to a spotty performance in a pre-season exhibition at Hofstra against the Long

Island Lacrosse Club. In the locker room afterwards, one of the Long Island players offered Steph a wood stick which was already out of favor with college players. I believe it was the only wood stick I saw the entire year. Steph took that gift and turned it into magic. He finished the season as the leading scorer in the country with 23 goals and 40 assists. It was his four goals and three and two from teammates Bob Rubeor and Dave White that led to a convincing 11-3 victory over Cornell that day. But that's not the story...

Brown now had a shot at its first outright Ivy title with a road game at Penn the most significant obstacle. In the meantime, Steph was following through with his career plans and was offered two possible dates for a mandatory Peace Corps orientation. His options were the week before the game with Penn or the weekend that would include the game at Dartmouth. At the same time, it was a realistic goal that he finish the season as Brown's alltime leading scorer. His teammates assumed he would simply make that decision until he came to the team with the generous offer that "I will do whatever you think is best." The team ultimately decided that we could beat Dartmouth without him and that we truly needed him to be properly prepared for the game at Penn. We went on to beat the Quakers in a close game 9-7, won at Dartmouth 15-6 and finished the season as undefeated Ivy League Champions.

In turn, Steph finished the season #2 on Brown's alltime list, only two points behind 1970 grad "Bullet" Bob Anthony. He spent his two Peace Corps years working with underserved children in Bogota, Colombia, and returned to New York City to begin a career at the Goddard Riverside Community Center. He spent 39 years at Goddard, including the last 19 as its Executive Director. He retired just this past February 10th.

My favorite sports book is Dean Smith's autobiography *A Coach's Life*. In the introduction he states that "there is great value in examining the athletic heart at the championship level." I have considered his insightful words often over the course of a long career. In this instance, the guy who least wanted to be thought of as a jock, provided one of the most profound examples of an athlete's heart at the championship level...of life.

1973 Brown teammates Jeff Wagner and Steph Russo

# 18

## An Unlikely Path to the Hall of Fame

I did not realize it was late in my final spring as the head coach at Brown University. I had gone over to Westminster School outside of Hartford to see one of our recruits, Dennis Fitzgibbons, a PG set to attend Brown in the fall. It was simply a courtesy call, as much as anything. It did not take long, however, to turn my attention unexpectedly to a wildly athletic, undersized, unorthodox and yet fearless lefthanded attackman. I may have wanted to get to know more about him but my attention was soon diverted again when I was offered the position at the University of Virginia. I had plenty to do that summer moving the family to Charlottesville and did not think too much more about the recruiting until walking into the office for the first time in late August. Marc VanArsdale had worked a year for Jim Adams and was already settled in the office that first day. When I greeted him with, "Marc, I have this wild little LH attackman I really like that no one knows about," he immediately responded with "Doug Knight!" Seems that Marc had seen Doug a year or two before at a Hobart camp and we, eerily, shared the same impression.

When I finally got a hold of Doug and we arranged to meet soon thereafter, I told him I thought he could be an excellent lacrosse player at Virginia. He looked at me like I had two heads

Michael, Timmy and Doug with David Curry, summer tournament 2012

and proceeded to inform me that he was a soccer/hockey player likely to play those two sports at a Division III school in New England. He said that he only played lacrosse because they made him do something in the spring. I told him to think about it and that we would talk again.

Meanwhile, heralded HS star attackman Michael Watson committed to Virginia and would join Tim Whiteley, who was a year ahead and already on campus. Long time and very successful St Paul's School coach Mitch Whiteley challenged me on more than one occasion with, "I hope you have someone good to play with Timmy and Michael." When I began to respond that I had this little attackman out of New England that I really liked, I could sense his skepticism.

By mid fall of his senior year (how's that for early recruiting!), I needed a decision from Doug and we slightly increased a minimum offer to nudge him away from Yale. Mike Waldvogel threw a bit of an "Ivy League hissy fit" and threatened to go to my Athletic Director to protest the pressure we were putting on Doug to decide. Believe me Mike, Doug was no Yalie and perhaps unwittingly, one of the finest attack trios in our game's history came together.

My early teams at Virginia were populated primarily with skilled, Maryland based players. Upperclassmen are always interested in the new players coming on board and ours were mildly intrigued when I continued to talk about this kid from NE. Unfortunately, Doug arrived on campus with some form of "Adirondack spotted fever" and was only physically able to attend about half the practices. When he was there, he could only just barely keep up with his new teammates. Doug, to this day, is the most one-handed player I have ever coached and while you might not think it unreasonable to have college attackmen switch hands during line drills, Doug could only barely function with the stick in his right hand. It was more than one of those upperclassmen who came to me to exclaim "I don't think so, Coach" about Doug's chances. No one (including me, perhaps) knew quite what to make of Doug during that first fall. Near to the end of that fall session, we scrimmaged Hampden-Sydney with our first and second years...almost from out of nowhere, Doug was all over that field that evening and had six goals in the first half. I can tell you that I smiled at all those upperclass jaws dropping again. The legend of Doug Knight was off and running...

I might still describe Doug in some variation of that first impression...athletic, unorthodox, just fearless. He could only really "fake left, go left" and those ACC defensemen would just be waiting for him on the corner. He dove over, under, around and would get brutalized while making one spectacular play after another. He led the nation with 58 goals in 1996, his junior year, and I can only recall that one of them might have been scored righthanded. He broke his stick the night before our opener against Syracuse in '96 and looked at me like, "what now?" I handed him mine with a "try this" and he had eight goals the next day. I can still recall Roy Simmons afterwards asking me, "Dom, who was that #7?" They took the dive out of the game the year after Doug graduated. He was selected the National Player of the Year in '96, 1st team AA again in '97 and was an iconic player of his generation. Doug, Michael and Timmy finished their careers #s 1, 2 & 3 as Virginia's alltime leading scorers.

All because of a courtesy call…

# 19

## Like Riding A Bike

In June of 2001, I went to the inaugural session of the Blue Chip Camp being held at McDonogh School to see a single player from a small high school in Central New Jersey. There were fewer than a hundred players in attendance and only a handful of college coaches who were paying attention. Although Matt Poskay had scored over 300 goals going into his senior year, the skeptics outnumbered the believers with regards to his college potential. He was a peculiar player. I never saw him dodge and he faced off with one leg extended straight behind. We offered him the last spot in the class (until we offered one to JJ Morrissey).

This modest high school student graduated from the McIntire School of Commerce at the University of Virginia in 2006. He was twice selected as an All-American, he was an Academic All-American and played key roles on National Championship teams in both 2003 and 2006. Matt went on to be a MLL All-Star in both 2007 and 2008 and was the League MVP in 2010. He spent the 2009 MLL season in recovery from testicular cancer that was diagnosed that spring.

Matt had an amazing playing career and I use the story of his journey whenever I find myself talking to young players. When I ask them if they would like to replicate his college experience, they respond with a resounding, "yes, of course." Well, here is the simple key that unlocks that door...Matt got up for breakfast every day. You mean "most days," "you don't mean Sunday mornings in college," "you mean like five days a week"...no, I mean every day. Go back and read through Matt's career, I am offering that to you...all you may have to do is agree to get up every morning for breakfast. I am not even saying that you can't go out but, you gotta get up! Think about that and consider how many young men are unwilling to make that trade-off.

Fast forward to the fall of 2016...my first fall in 42 years without lacrosse and Matt entering his 6th year as the head coach at Wagner College. Matt was one of my favorite players, someone who possessed that rare combination of confidence and personality. Always respectful, he gave it as good as he got from me on the practice field and I treasured those exchanges. We probably talked twice a week throughout his coaching career and those conversations and his personality helped him survive the incremental growth of the Wagner program.

It was during one of these late summer phone calls that Matt mentioned he was short a member of his coaching staff. When I suggested that I might be able to come by a couple of times to help out in some way, he asked if they might issue a press release making that announcement. We both agreed to hold off on the release but we immediately scheduled a couple of visits when I could make back-to-back sessions. When I began to ask if he would like me to stand off to the side and make some observations, or to get a little more involved, etc., he cut me off with: "No, no, I want you out there, let them have it." To Matt, his staff and his players' great credit, I found myself comfortable almost immediately. I could have easily been on a field at Brown or Virginia and it was only 15 minutes in when the entire team dropped for push-ups when someone went offsides in a drill. That was like riding a bike.

If I lived closer to Staten Island, I might have Matt issue that press release. As it is, I will try to help whenever I can. I was impressed with the attentiveness of the Wagner players, their enthusiasm and their athleticism; I think they are onto something. I think they liked doing the pushups!

Matt Poskay, May 2006

# 20

# Football and Lacrosse

The Patriot's Chris Hogan is not the only NFL player with lacrosse-playing roots. Philadelphia Eagles defensive end Chris Long will also be making his second consecutive trip to the Super Bowl next week. I first became aware of Chris when he and my son played on the same Pop Warner football team soon after we moved to Charlottesville. Chris also played lacrosse while a student at St Ann's Belfield. UVA recruit James King was also on that St Ann's team and I may have seen them play 3-4 times in their senior spring. The truth is I am not sure I ever saw a ball actually in Chris' stick during all that time but he was sure fun to track when the ball was on the ground. There may have been as many penalties as goals scored in many of those games. There were many skeptics about his college football potential but he was a dynamo in the weight room. Presently, it is his courage on social justice issues and humanitarian efforts that truly distinguish these later years of his career.

Before Chris Long, there was another UVA defensive end that travelled a very different early path but also had a long, decorated NFL career. I arrived at the New England Top 150 Lacrosse Camp at Williams College for a short visit in the summer of 1994. Upon arrival, one of the coaches mentioned that there was a camper who wanted to talk with me and I was happy to oblige. As the following session drew to a close a young man came across the field while blotting out the sun. He stuck out his hand and said "Coach Starsia, my name is Patrick Kerney and I would like to talk with you about the University of Virginia." My response to this 6'6"/230lb specimen, with the old white arm pads and biceps bulging through the straps, was simply, "Son, I have no idea who you are but we are very interested in talking with you about the University of Virginia!" I came to find out that Patrick wrestled and played football and lacrosse at the Taft School in Connecticut.

It was always a bit of an oversimplification to say that I just looked for athletes in the recruiting but I was looking for guys who thought they could play football at Virginia. I had a couple who were close—Mark Farnham, Brett Hughes, Steve Holmes and Chris LaPierre—some who were FB players in lacrosse player's bodies—Darren Muller, Ryan Curtis and Walt Cataldo—a couple who had the tools but not the temperament—Rhamel and Shamel Bratton—and only one who was actually a much better college football player than he ever would have been a lacrosse player. Patrick Kerney was just too big for us and wound up better suited rushing the passer than covering some small, quick college middie.

Early in the recruiting, Patrick asked for permission to walk on the football team at UVA. I had a number of these requests over the years and always said yes. You come to college, you need to make some of these decisions for yourself and in every prior case, the players would last 3-4 days at practice before realizing that a walk-on lacrosse player was not going to be handed the ball in a scrimmage nor be allowed to tackle one of the returning veterans. With Patrick in mind, I went to the football coaches and told them that "I won't pretend to tell you your business but I may have one here." They looked at me like I had two heads, with an expression of "yeah, right." Film of Patrick's senior year at Taft was very inconclusive because of the quality of play and his missing most of the year with an injured knee.

Recruited walk-ons in football are invited to the start of practice in early August; others do not see the field until the start of school in September. I talked the coaches into giving Patrick a shot in August but anticipated that he might have been in my office a week later having had enough of all that. Instead, it was the head football coach, George Welsh, who informed me shortly thereafter that Patrick might be "the best freshman in the class." A mere two weeks later, Patrick was one of the few true freshman to participate in Virginia's first game of the 1995 season at the University of Michigan. He went from classes on a Saturday morning and a crowd of about 300 at the Taft Homecoming to 108,000 and a game decided on the very last play in the Big House in less than a year.

Patrick enrolled at Virginia on the smallest scholarship we are allowed to provide having someone designated as a scholarship athlete. He lettered that fall and the football coach told him that he was expected at spring practice. When Patrick told Coach Welsh that "I came to Virginia to play lacrosse and I am playing lacrosse," Welsh told me that he respected Patrick even more for sticking to his guns. Patrick lettered in lacrosse that spring for a team that lost in OT of the NCAA Finals. We would joke that Patrick was always going to be the first off the bus when we arrived at a visitor's site and I remember walking Coach Pressler over to the practice field just to look at Pat the day before our game with Duke. Following that first year, football put Pat on a full scholarship and it was not a request for him to participate in spring football in his second year. Pat came back out to lacrosse after spring practice in '97.

Those few weeks in '97 were the end of Pat's college lacrosse career. He began to realize his potential in football and needed to eat, lift and put on weight. Like Chris Long, Patrick burned "white hot" in the weight room in those years and went from 240 to 255 pounds between his second and third year and was almost 270 as a senior. He also worked our lacrosse camp in those summers and I am sure his standing outside the camp store and charging campers to hang from his arms was some level of NCAA violation.

Even though we missed Patrick's easy temperament on a daily basis, it was a joy to watch his football career unfold. He was a first team All-American defensive end as a senior, led the conference in sacks, was the ACC Co-Defensive Player of the Year and wound up as a first round draft choice of the Atlanta Falcons. He was already in Atlanta working out when school ended but found his way to College Park, MD, to join us for the 1999 Final Four weekend. It was Patrick's senior class that led the way to UVA's first NCAA Championship in 27 years. He was, in spirit, always a member of our program and that team.

A couple of weeks following the championship, I was speaking with Patrick on the phone and he informed me that "Yesterday, Coach, I had $27 in my checking account...this morning $1,000,027!" The Falcons had direct deposited his signing bonus. Patrick went on to an 11 year NFL career with the Falcons and the Seahawks, played in the 2004 Pro Bowl (his jersey hangs in my office), missed only 7 games in those 11 years, earned his MBA at Columbia and presently works for the NFL office in NYC...not bad for a walk-on from the Western NE Prep League.

# "Walk Humbly, Be Truthful"

I was out in Missouri recently, working with a notable high school program. After a meeting with the team, an underclassmen came up and asked me "what is the single, defining characteristic of outstanding individual leadership"? He put me on the spot but the word I chose that day, fearlessness, might still be my choice. It takes an exceptional person to be able to stand up to his teammates, define the unyielding requirements for success and, in the next moment, walk into the coach's office on behalf of those same teammates.

The exercise leads me to consider the response if the young man had asked me the single determinant for exceptional team chemistry/performance. What is the distinguishing characteristic of those teams who have played closest to their potential? All those teams had great leadership but the formula for success, the "secret sauce" that created an environment for those leaders to influence their teammates was honesty among all the participants. I would tell you that the inverse is also true. During seasons in which we may have struggled, a lack of trust among the team and the staff was often the culprit.

I find myself preoccupied with this topic as I consider the influence on young people of the deterioration of honesty in the public discourse. Anyone who has raised a child knows that young children mimic what they see and hear. I am not asking Charles Barkley to raise my children but ALL those in the public arena bear some responsibility to set a moral example. It is of even greater concern to me in this historical moment that an impressionable young person may come to believe that a legitimate ascendancy to power can be obtained following an unprincipled pathway. What effect will this present environment have on our next generation of leaders?

The German writer Goethe said "truth is contrary to our nature, not so error, and this for a very simple reason; truth demands that we should recognize ourselves as limited, error flatters us that, in one way or another, we are unlimited," and Thomas Jefferson said "honesty is the first chapter in the Book of Wisdom." Becoming a man or woman of value and wisdom can be an arduous journey but it is built on truthfulness. Becoming a great lacrosse player (truthfulness to oneself), a great team leader (truthfulness to your peers) and part of a great organization (truthfulness to the environment) is worth the considerable sacrifices that may be required. Truth is liberating but it can also be unwieldy. Lying always requires more lying, "a liquid that oozes everywhere" writes Michael Rosenberg and any short term benefit will make the long term journey required of your personal legacy all the more difficult to navigate. It all works together and you will never be a true leader if you lie to teachers, academic coordinators, coaches, parents, peers, etc…ever.

I only began playing lacrosse as a freshman in college. One of the first players that made an impression on me was an unorthodox attackman from Freeport, New York. Paul Wehrum played crease attack for SUNY Cortland in the early 70's when they were one of the top programs in all of college lacrosse. He played attack with a six foot stick and had a knack for grabbing those high feeds that was nearly unstoppable. He went on to win 8 National Championships as the head coach at Herkimer Community College, is presently the coach at Union and was inducted into the National Hall of Fame in 1999. I heard Paul speak at the National Coach's convention around 2003 and he said something so simply eloquent that never left me. He talked about the culture around his team and the rules they live by. I should say "rule" because they have just the one…"don't lie." He mentioned that they had some issues and that he debated trying to cover all the possible infractions. In the end, the only thing that truly mattered to him was his relationship to the players, their taking responsibility for their lives and their ability to trust one another. He finally told them that the only non-negotiable was "lie to me and you're off the team." Paul built a Hall of Fame career on the unconditional premise.

I am hopeful that we will emerge from this moment in our history stronger for the turmoil and reflection. Don't let your judgment be clouded by murky visions of power and convenience. If your good name and your word come to mean something, you will be something. Truthfulness is a zero sum game and if you are willing to live and play by that standard, you will find yourself a better student, friend, brother, sister, teammate, one of Albert Einstein's "persons of value." Treat it as a New Year's resolution if you like, but it is not too late to start, today. I would suggest to any young players who aspire to greatness that alongside a commitment to the fundamentals of the game, a strong academic performance and a dedication to your overall athletic development, that you remain mindful of Gandhi's guideline to future goals..."be truthful, gentle and fearless." I am not sure the Mahatma ever watched Hopkins/Maryland live at Homewood but I can assure you that following his recommendation will improve your circumstance, on and off the lacrosse field.

# LACROSSE

# Mental Toughness

*It is about to be that time of the year in our sport when a little mental toughness is required of all participants. As the start of the lacrosse season has slowly migrated into January, players, coaches, managers, trainers and fans find themselves in a survival mode as they force themselves through practice and games. What are the characteristics of those who will endure the early season, thrive in the daily battles and flourish in reaction to the competitive challenges? Let's examine the topic.*

I received a call about a year ago from Marquette coach Joe Amplo asking if I could come out to Milwaukee to consult with them about an effort to start an inner city lacrosse program. There was strong interest from the University president and the local chamber of commerce to find a way to connect with underserved, young urban men and women. I was happy to oblige and looked forward to my first visit to this emerging Midwestern lacrosse outpost. Joe met me at the airport and offered a tour of Marquette's lacrosse facilities. It did not take long, however, since the Golden Eagles don't have a locker room nor indoor practice facility, barely have a stadium, lack a dedicated meeting space and just procured adequate offices. Did I mention that they had just beaten Denver for the second year in a row, captured their second consecutive Big East title and were headed for a return trip to the NCAA Tournament? This all in their fifth year of existence.

When I asked Joe how all that was possible, his straightforward reply was "we recruit kids for whom all those other things are not important." While I am not sure there are enough of those particular prospects, for whom a visit to the facilities at OSU, ND and UMICH won't turn heads, Marquette has clearly found a formula for their own success. They have broadened the definition of toughness in our lacrosse lexicon. Wait a second, lacrosse is a private school sport, played in Garden City with guys in polo shirts! You might want to think twice about that characterization as you consider practicing lacrosse outdoors in Wisconsin in Jan, February and March. Let's talk about mental toughness and its relationship to success.

If you asked any competitive athlete how he would like to be described, the word "tough" would emerge consistently near the top of the list. The definition and concept of toughness has changed in my lifetime. I grew up in a time when salt pills, limited hydration, up/downs in the searing heat, daily live Oklahoma tackling drills and coaches screaming derogatory comments at me and my teammates were almost a requirement to make us tough enough to play high school football. I recall struggling with that connection but not questioning its wisdom. Try to imagine a football coach in these present days following Bear Bryant's example with his first Texas A & M team told in the blistering novel *Junction Boys*.

I do not have all the physical nor psychological data on a topic like this but I am resolute in my belief that players do not need to be put into physical peril nor encouraged to act accordingly in order to identify and enhance athletic toughness. I have always been much less impressed with those lacrosse players who would seem to define their lives by being primarily physical…swinging your stick, always looking for the big hit, act tough or happy to tell you how tough they are, etc…than I am with those who simply do the right thing over and over. We are all drawn to the stories of those who get knocked down, get back up and have the fortitude to persevere. Early in my career, I came across a quote by Jim Lohrer that resonated to my core "consistency is the ultimate measure of mental toughness in an athlete and is the distinguishing characteristic of a champion." My coaching philosophy over a long career was built on that premise.

You do not have to hit someone like an NFL outside linebacker, take a punch like a professional boxer or stare down personal endangerment like those in the military to meet the requirement for mental toughness. We see glowing examples of mental toughness every day, all around us…if you get up for work every day, care for your family, love your mate, do your job consistently well, you may be mentally tough enough. If you are a person that family, friends and teammates can turn to when life seems about to go off the rails, you may be tougher than you think. Winston Churchill said, "When you are going through hell, keep going." We may not picture Churchill in this literal context but those who emerge at the end of that journey may be the quiet disciples of that quality.

It bears repeating that consistency is the trademark characteristic of toughness. Doing the right thing over and over again, doing it when it needs to be done. A player who can't or won't adjust his fundamentals to hit a big shot more than once in a while, the player who gets a tough ground ball once in a while, who gives in on defense when he tires, who looks for short cuts in the weight room or who picks his spots in the conditioning, will

Matt Ward and Chris Rotelli, Alumni Game, 2008

not likely be the one you turn to when a game is being decided. Coaches are the role models here. Are you organized every day? Do you have your practice plan up on the board in the locker room? Do you hold your players to consistent standards of practice performance and behavior? Are you early onto the field? Are you excited every day? Do you visit with the non-starters regularly? Do you carry the ball bag? This is not a model that will necessarily be recognized on the first day but players will begin to strive to match your strong, quiet bearing.

Tough players have a resilient spirit. They absolutely accept failure as part of the process. They are convinced that getting knocked to the ground reflects effort and growth and often come up smiling. They manage their discomfort in every instance. These players forget about a shot the very moment it leaves their stick and are immediately on to the next play.

This resilient spirit leads to poise and unbreakable body language. The mentally tough do not take careless fouls, they don't retaliate in the heat of a moment, they play through pain, they don't blame teammates and they do not exhibit athletic uncertainty. At halftime of our 2003 regular season game with Syracuse in the Dome, Chris Rotelli sat in the middle of the locker room bleeding from a "walnut" swelling on his forehead. With a sore shoulder and his fresh stitches, he went out and scored the winner late in a one-goal game. In the larger team context, Virginia had not won a national championship in 27 years when we found ourselves up three goals at halftime in the 1999 Finals. I told the team as we were about to exit the locker room on this sweltering day that "Syracuse will make a run at us here late in the game fellas, no matter what, run everywhere, run to the faceoff line, run to the bench, don't give an inch." It was no small matter and we needed a strong, clear signal of our intent as we exited the locker room. The Orange closed to within one with three minutes to go but we rose up and made the plays.

Resiliency, poise, body language and a little sense of humor doesn't hurt. Mentally tough athletes often have that little devilish smile that seems to indicate that they know something that the rest of us don't recognize. They might be trash talkers but they don't give in to it, never affects their play. What I may miss the most about coaching is the give and take on the practice field with those special athletes who give it back (respectfully) as good as they were getting it from me. Smiling helps you cope.

Poise also refers to taking responsibility. I have always had a simple set of rules for players and one of them is "don't whine." Someone put it very well, "you take what life gives you, you make something out of it, everything else is just whining." The coaches are screwing you, the professors don't like you, your parents aren't fair, your stick doesn't work…it's truly not about any of that and, even if it was true (some of it not impossible to imagine), you need to persevere in spite of those issues. Players who come into my office and imply that they are not playing more simply because I don't like them, I tell them all, "tough luck." Even if it was true and it hardly ever is, I'm the head coach and you are going to have to find a way to succeed in spite of this personal dilemma. I also tell them that putting the best players on the field is not nearly the most difficult thing I do. Don't whine.

Selflessness is another important characteristic of the mentally tough. Booker Washington said "If you want to lift yourself up, lift up someone else." Mentally tough players don't even consider the first part of that statement. "How can I lift others?"…oh, by lifting myself?… OK, I'll do that!. They live to serve the team and those around them, without hesitation. In every daily endeavor, we will ultimately improve our own lives more when we put the welfare of others before our own. I truly admired Tim Tebow's description of the quality he was looking for in a life partner, someone with a "servant's heart." If you want to be a great coach, a great player, a leader, a captain, a good husband and father, the most mentally tough among us come to all those circumstances with a servant's heart. Tim Tebow may not have the arm for the NFL nor be able to hit a big league curveball but, he is one of the great leaders in college football history and a poster boy for toughness.

While we have talked about the qualities and characteristics of toughness, its manifestations in practice come in different shapes and sizes. I would put Greg Louganis beside Ronnie Lott on any high end of the scale, Kerri Shrug alongside Willis Reed, Nick Saban and Dabo Swinney, Lindsey Vonn, Jackie Robinson, the late Dale Earnhardt and on and on. The 1980 US Hockey Team endured Herb Brooks and coalesced around a commitment to toughness and determination. The 2011 Virginia Lacrosse team went from talented to tough midway through that season and persevered in spite of being down three goals with three minutes to play in the 1st round of the NCAA playoffs, down three goals early in the quarterfinals and having lost 4 of their top 5 players going into the semifinal. It definitely required a certain toughness for the 2017 Maryland men's team to deal with the ghosts of 42 years of championships past.

How do we encourage and build toughness in our athletes and our teams? We need to explore other avenues than simply putting our athletes in additional situations of physical vulnerability. In the final third of that 2011 season, we went to live GB's every day in an attempt to emphasize a requirement for toughness. My heart leapt when our captain went down in a heap during this drill in a practice at the Stadium the day before the semifinal with Denver. You might get tougher but you are likely to run out of players if you load up on live GB's and 1 v 1's. In fact, the winningest college football of all time with 489 wins is John Gagliardi from St John's University in Collegeville, Minnesota. Using unconventional methods, Gagliardi's philosophy includes no yelling, no whistles, no sprints, no calisthenics and does not allow ANY live tackling in practice. He recalled in a recent article that they had not made one since 1958!

You reinforce the qualities of mental toughness before you step onto the field. Insist on attention to detail, set standards and hold the players accountable. Keep the locker room neat, no meals in the locker room immediately before practice (plan your day better!), finish reps in the weight room and on the practice field. My common refrain to players is that "the fruit is at the bottom." You need to dig down in order to get to the fruit, get through all that yogurt to get to the good stuff! Whether it is the very end of a drill, a full extension of an exercise in the weight room or the final repetition in the running. Make sure we are finishing our drills because we want to make that play at the late critical moment on game day. Be on time for study hall and prepared for tutors. West Genesee has taught us the value of dressing properly for practice and games. A little touch of self-discipline, a little piece of being mentally tougher.

You truly establish the culture of your team on the practice field. Let them know that when they cross that line, they are ready to work. Chin straps are buttoned, have a plan for pre-practice shooting, insist on lining up properly for stretching and sticks ready for the workout. Practice starts and there are "no palms up" (body language), no offsides in practice, no cursing allowed, no pushes in the back, no retaliation fouls EVER, finish drills and run the first and last sprint equally hard. There are others and you should identify your own list and implant your own athletic priorities. Failure to comply and the whole team pays the price (something firm but sensible to get their attention, to make your point). Rather than thinking about additional "tough" drills, emphasize to the players that "every" drill contributes to mental toughness.

You establish standards in the locker room and on the practice field and demand attention to detail and consistent execution. Young men want discipline in their lives. They may moan at first, complain about a strict adherence to minor routines but they will come to appreciate a consistent, even-handed policy. In addition, the mentally tough among them will flourish in this atmosphere. Whether it is athletics, business or simply the rest of one's life, we all need a little mental toughness to get through the events we encounter on our daily journey.

*"Nothing is easy, and nothing does itself. Character and action are everything."*

Washington A. Roebling

*"That which we obtain too easily, we esteem too lightly. It is dearness only that gives everything its true value. Heaven knows how to put a proper price on its goods."*

Thomas Paine

*"Whatsoever thy hand findeth to do, do it with thy might."*

Scripture

*"It's better to decide wrongly, than weakly; if you're weak, you're likely to be wrong anyway."*

Bill Parcells

*"Genius at first is little more than a great capacity for receiving discipline."*

George Eliot

*"I am a Shawnee. My forefathers were warriors. Their son is a warrior...from my tribe I take nothing. I am the maker of my own fortune."*

Tecumseh

*"As life is action and passion, so a man must participate in the action and passion of his times, at peril of being judged not to have lived."*

Oliver Wendell Holmes

*"[It is] the last of human freedoms: to choose one's attitude under any circumstances."*

Viktor E. Frankl

*"For those to whom much is given, much is required."*

John F Kennedy, 1961
(from Luke 12:48)

# No Big Games

One of the coaching questions I am asked most frequently is establishing the ability to achieve and maintain a consistent level of performance. We would all like our teams to play their best every game and are desperate to avoid those sub-par performances. One of the great joys of our sport at the college level is that most of the best teams play each other during the regular season. It is a feast for fans but is a challenge for coaches and players. During most of my time at Virginia, we had a stretch of consecutive weekends that began with Syracuse at the end of February and proceeded through Cornell, Notre Dame, Hopkins, Maryland, North Carolina, Duke and the ACC Tournament in succession. How do you go through a run of games of this caliber and maintain the emotional and physical edge required to succeed?

It was early in my career when I first became aware of John Gagliardi, the head football coach at St John's University in central Minnesota. The winningest college football coach in history (489 wins) built a program and a career on an unlikely philosophy called "Winning with No's." In his system, there was no calisthenics, no sprints, no tackling dummies, no whistles, no live tackling (ever) and...no big games. It is certainly hard to imagine most of the football coaches in my lifetime agreeing to abide by such a radical ideology. At the same time, we are all such copy cats and football coaches are simply choosing to ignore the most successful formula.

I did not read anything more about the concept of "no big games" but just that simple expression seemed a revelation. As coaches, we are always talking with our charges about getting ready for a big game. We want to play our best, Cornell is a "big game" but, what happens when the game ends and we have Notre Dame coming up? That is a big game too, is it bigger than Cornell? Players want truth, they want to be spoken to plainly and honestly. I think any coach would struggle making a convincing argument that you had big game after big game coming up one after the other throughout a long season. In addition, how do you make the argument for a midweek game between Hopkins and Maryland?

The concept of no big games became a liberating philosophy that addressed more than just game day emotional preparation. If there were no big games allowed, it was not complicated to elevate that idea to the next level and suggest that no day was more important than any other. By saying that "we want to have a good practice today," are you suggesting that you won't require that tomorrow? I realize that would not be anyone's intention but, again, what are your players hearing? "No big games, no big days" means that every game and every day is the most important. We want to achieve and maintain a level of daily performance that will help us reach our final goals. I aspire to have a team that gets after it every day and expects of themselves to play their best no matter the name on the opponent's jersey.

At the same time, I completely understand and accept that walking into the Dome produced a different level of anticipation and excitement. However, we would never allow any talk of a "big game" throughout the week, either among ourselves or with the press. The players knew what was going on, it helped us focus on the daily effort. I do remember distinctly, being asked the morning of the National Championship game in 2003 by assistant coach David Curry…"how about today, Coach, big game today?" "Nope, David," with a smile… "No Big Games Allowed."

*"The smart take from the strong."*

Pete Carril

*"Try not to become a man of success but rather try to become a man of value."*

Albert Einstein

*"Leadership is actually more akin to consistency of authenticity across stressful environments."*

Michael Gervais

*"Risk more than others think is safe. Care more than others think is wise. Dream more than others think is practical. Expect more than others think is possible."*

Cadet Maxim, US Military

# A Little Chaos Can Be Helpful

It has always been a great joy for me to have young coaches ask for advice, particularly in the area of finding the balance between the requirements of family and the necessities of our profession. It can certainly seem overwhelming to consider a formula that makes it all work. I was the head coach at Brown in 1985 with four children under four years of age, two with special needs, two who were gifted, talented and stubborn and a wife who shortly thereafter went back to work. Frankly, some of it is a blur but I tell young couples not to dwell on the daily, practical application. Generally, I would leave them with "don't think about it too much, if you love each other and this is the life you want to lead, you can be confident that you will figure out a way to make it work."

A significant part of the formula for success here is the accompanying understanding that with each child comes an increased parental appreciation for the value of chaos in their lives. You might not let the first one out of your sight…by two, three, four and so on, you kinda know where they are most of the time. I would argue that this time-honored parental evolution gives the adults a chance to survive and the children an environment in which to thrive. I am also going to try and turn around and make an argument that our teams would benefit from an application of the same principle.

I have always taken exception to the declarative statement that "defense wins championships." In fluid sports like basketball and lacrosse, you HAVE TO score to win. It is not a coincidence that 11 of the past 18 D1 National Champions have been Duke (3), Syracuse (4) and Virginia (4), teams that play the entire field. Notre Dame has been close during this period but now seems even closer, corresponding to Matt Kavanagh's influence on how the Fighting Irish are now willing to play on offense. It would be my very benign observation that Coach Corrigan was dragged "kicking and screaming" into this new chaotic world and they are even more dangerous now overall. It is my very strong belief that it is "defense and offense that win championships."

How do we create an environment in which players learn to execute going up and down the field? Two things, I am talking about both offensive and defensive players thriving in these fluid situations. There is nothing more difficult to defend than teams that attack unexpectedly and unpredictably. We tend to think of these situations from an offensive perspective but, generally, there is a heavier price to pay at the defensive end. Second, I am not talking about just being good in transition. We all practice transition O and D and, if we have the athletes, we want to be good in transition. What I am trying to get to is a greater sense of creativity in our athletes, an ability to react and think on their feet. I also believe that creative thinking requires a greater sense of responsibility from the players and courage from the coaches. It takes courage to be innovative and the less coaching ego, the better. The cynics among us would smirk when agreeing that Roy (Simmons) and John's (Desko) Syracuse teams were "not overcoached." However, it took a bold, innovative approach to create the environment where players of that character and talent were encouraged to think outside the box. I am

With Head Coach Cliff Stevenson on the sideline at Brown, 1980

certain that some of those teams would have won with a different coach and a different approach but you would be completely missing the point if you took for granted the improvisational nuance of what was going on in the Dome. If they were actually making it up as they went along, how could you possibly prepare to play them?

I have thought about this a great deal and I sincerely hope I can articulate this idea effectively. These creative skills need to be trained like any others. Especially later in my career, I found myself standing on the practice field during fullfield unsettled drills with a picture in my mind of how each repetition would conclude itself. It occurred to me that if knew how a drill was to play out properly, a successful conclusion would simply be my pre-ordained execution of the drill. A good job of communicating my intent for the drill and an efficient processing by the players has some teaching value but, were the players actually having to think for themselves? A light went off…was it possible to develop drills in which you cannot orchestrate or predict the sequencing and ending? Yes, the very ending, I know…we want the ball to go in or not to go in but, how about all the variables and spontaneity that got us there?

Oliver Wendell Holmes said, "Man's mind, once stretched by a new idea, never regains its original dimensions." The development of this creative improvisation requires an environment of chaos and unpredictability. Our job as coaches is to train our players to identify and select the best tactical options in a constantly evolving and, oftentimes, physically demanding setting. We are constantly searching for that moment when our players make the right choice without thinking, anticipate and react without overtly visible clues and lift the others around them.

How do we get to this place? I played for Cliff Stevenson at Brown U. Cliff's basic practice philosophy was simply to scrimmage and shoot and we did that every day. We argued about this (I was also his assistant for 8 years) and he would say to me that if we had equal sets of athletes and I could do whatever we wanted in practice and all he would do is scrimmage and shoot, that he would beat us every time. Along the way, he never got enough credit for developing players who loved practice and learned to think on their feet. Frankly, I recognize some of the method in that madness much moreso now than I did when I was younger and convinced I knew all the answers. I have no issue recommending to coaches that they develop a little more of Cliff's philosophy. Scrimmage a little more, let them play, let them figure it out on their own. Scramble it with a new ball flying in anywhere on every whistle, with a fifteen second shot clock, with only two steps allowed with the ball in your stick, with two defensemen and three attackmen at both ends, etc. In each case, we are trying to create chaotic situations that would be hard to script and require innovative interpretation by the participants. In turn, learning to deal with chaos, to endure in a chaotic environment, encourages both independent thinking and a competitive survival instinct. We are looking to create athletes, soldiers, business people who embrace the former navy seal Richard Marcinko ethos, "I will always be easy to find: I will be in the center of the battle."

My favorite drill at Virginia was a fullfield unsettled scramble. Groups of attackmen, defensemen and goalies in opposite colors at both ends of the field, all the white middies with one assistant on one sideline, all the blue with another assistant on the other. I am patrolling the middle of the field with a whistle and a bag of balls. The drill can start with either goalie picking up a ball. The blue goalie picks it up, one pass below the restraining line is required, the coach with the blue middies sends out 1, 2 or 3 of them…as soon as the first pass is made, they are free to attack the field. At the same time, the coach of the white team sends out 1, 2 or 3 middies of his own. We might have gone into the day's practice telling the coaches that we wanted to work on all even fullfield transition (he sends out 1, you send out 1, etc.) or, our emphasis that day might be more uneven fullfield work (he sends out 2 to offense, you send out 1). The point is that the coaches can, essentially, send out whatever numbers they like and if they are making unpredictable decisions, the players will truly need to identify and react. If the ball hits the ground or goes out of bounds, the coaches can pull off any number of players (or leave them on) going up and down the field. The kicker is that every time I blow a whistle, I also throw a new ball into play. It encourages the attack and defense at the other end to move up toward the midline because I might just drop a new ball right there. I describe my role (mostly to myself!) as "Johnny Appleseed." Halfway through the drill switch the middies from one sideline to the other, it changes the flow for both units. The drill is an exercise in organized chaos, generally raises the energy level in practice and can become highly competitive. If you have the luxury of a scoreboard on your practice field, put up 15 minutes and keep the score…I believe you will begin to see traces of accountability, poise and creative thinking. It was the advertising icon George Lois who said "Creativity can solve almost any problem. The creative act, the defeat of habit by high originality, overcomes everything."

I hope this makes some sense for everyone. As with most things, the truth generally lies closer to the middle in these situations. There is a requirement and value for repetition in team sports but there is a potential for growth here for our players and a coach's daily search is for the appropriate balance. The stakes have risen in recent years, the tendency is to over control. Be mindful. Looking for and allowing some chaos in any environment requires some courage and a level of confidence on the part of a coach, a parent or someone in a business setting. Let me encourage you to dedicate some part of your weekly meeting with employees or lacrosse staff to hearing completely new ideas from everyone. Encourage them to think outside the box, that "everything is in play," up is down, wrong is right, etc. Your biggest issue may still be convincing them to suggest something they don't think you will want to hear. When I came to appreciate the liberating effect of acknowledging that I simply did not have all the answers, it freed me up try some different things. Keep an open mind, don't be afraid of a little chaos, a little disruptive innovation. Encourage your employees to help you search the universe for new ideas. What may be unsettling initially may pay big dividends for your business, employees, the players and for your team.

March 28, 1984 v. Adelphi

*"Success doesn't come to you…you go to it."*

Marva Collins

*"There is no delight in owning anything unshared."*

Seneca

*"Even if you are on the right track, you'll get run over if you just sit there."*

Will Rogers

*"There is a choice you have to make, in everything you do. So keep in mind that in the end, the choice you make, makes you."*

John Wooden

*"Everyone has a plan until they get hit."*

Mike Tyson

*"Action springs not from thought, but from a readiness for responsibility."*

Dietrich Bonhoeffer

*"You must be interested in finding the best way, not in having your own way."*

John Wooden

*"Never doubt that a small group of thoughtful, committed citizens can change the world; indeed, it's the only thing that ever has."*

Margaret Meade

# There is No Deserve

In the climactic scene from the movie *Unforgiven,* laconic Clint Eastwood bursts into the bar and methodically shoots all the bad guys, including the film's chief antagonist, Gene Hackman. Still alive, with Eastwood standing over him pointing a shotgun, Hackman exclaims, "I don't deserve to die like this." To which Eastwood calmly responds, "It's got nothing to do with deserve" and proceeds to pull the trigger.

It's funny how often a fleeting moment, an expression, a comment, something you read or saw will resonate profoundly with one person or another. I always was a Clint fan and likely saw that movie close to its release date in 1992. I left Brown in the summer of 1992 and I thought of that movie dialogue often, especially in my early years in Charlottesville. Virginia had not won a national championship in twenty years and we were being constantly reminded that we were "not tough enough" and that it might never happen. We found ourselves in OT of the National Championship game in '94, made the right play on defense but had a deflected ball trickle directly through to Hall of Famer Kevin Lowe who drilled the winner. We returned to the Final Four in '95 but got manhandled by Roy Colsey and a Syracuse team that we had beaten earlier in the season. In '96, we found ourselves back in the championship game and down three goals in the fourth quarter. We came storming back to force overtime and found ourselves in the huddle getting ready to go out for the extra period. We used two faceoff guys throughout that year and throughout that game and I was not certain who would take that important draw. From across the huddle, 6'3 and rugged, David Wren made eye contact with me and mouthed the words "I got this one." What more could you want from an athlete in that situation than that very stoic reaction? I remember thinking distinctly "we're in!" Well, David could not have lost that faceoff any quicker and we never touched the ball. It found its way to Jesse Hubbard, Hall of Fame, case closed.

I do not want to go any further without saying that I will always admire David for his reaction at that critical moment. Michael Jordan always talks about all the shots he missed in between the ones that we remember him making. After 42 years coaching college lacrosse, I can speak to the secret of winning close games...are you leaning in? It is having good players who are willing to step up at the moment that a game is being decided. How many times was it Brian Carroll or Steele Stanwick or, now, Conor Canizzaro or Matt Rambo who find the ball in their stick at the critical moment? It is not a coincidence.

Who will win this weekend? Having those clutch players in your colors will certainly increase your chances. The University of Maryland has had a lot of those guys since they last raised the championship trophy in 1975. Not quite enough, you need to complete the play. It might take a save if you have the lead, it might take a faceoff, a groundball and a shot, if the score is tied. I cannot recall the setting where I heard Richie Moran say to his

Cornell team, "When you cross that line, you make something happen." Every coach should be sending his team out this weekend with those same instructions.

The results of these games can oftentimes seem so arbitrary, so cruel. For Denver, OSU, Towson and, especially for the Terps, there is no deserve in sports…only DO.

Good luck.

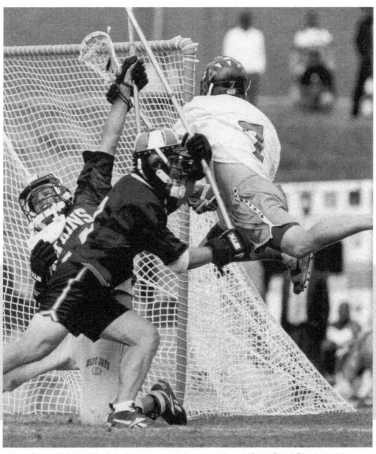

Doug Knight, Virginia '97, versus Johns Hopkins, NCAA Semi Finals 1996

*"Your ethical muscle grows stronger every time you choose right over wrong."*

Price Pritchett

*"If I had six hours to chop down a tree, I'd spend the first four hours sharpening the axe."*

Abe Lincoln

*"Those who believe they can and those who believe they can't...are both right."*

Henry Ford

*"Success is sweet, but it usually has the scent of sweat about it."*

Anonymous

*"Why do they not teach you that time is a finger snap and an eye blink, and that you should not allow a moment to pass you by without taking joyous, ecstatic note of it, not wasting a single moment of its swift, breakneck current."*

Pat Conroy

# 26

## Throw a Ball That Catches Itself

As we enter the summer camp/tournament season, I thought I might offer some hints to young players with aspirations. It will be hot and it may be taxing, fair enough, but still, show some enthusiasm, engage your teammates, be supportive of their success, listen to your coaches, do the little things (hustle after GB's, ride, etc.)...communicate on defense (everyone can do that!)... don't be afraid to stand out from your other very cool club buddies and most importantly, demonstrate (or develop) an ability to pass the ball.

One of the few positive memories that remain with me following the 2016 political experience was hearing someone say, "you are not only responsible for what you say, you are also responsible for what people hear." Unexpectedly, I was struck in a profound way on both a personal and professional level.

I loved my father dearly but I grew up listening to him use a coarse language to describe people or different situations. I may have been tone deaf early in my life and it caught me by surprise when I became uncomfortable with him talking the same way around my own children. When I admonished him, the common refrain would be "I didn't mean it that way." It really didn't matter what you meant, Dad, what mattered was what people heard.

Yowzer, how does this relate to lacrosse? Well, becoming a great passer follows the same paradigm. I had a defenseman at Virginia who grew up playing hockey in New England (are you listening Matt Lovejoy?). He was especially good with the ball around his feet and could throw the ball effectively from sidearm and below. The problem was that even his well-thrown balls were hard to catch. When a middie is running up the field wondering whether he is about to have his head taken off, where the clearing spaces are and whether he may wind up with a shot at the other end, there are not enough brain cells left to track a rising fastball from across the field. He needs to see the ball early and he needs it delivered simply, to a good spot.

The great passers of my coaching lifetime, Tim Goldstein, Tim Nelson, Darren Lowe, Ryan Boyle, Conor Gill and others, threw balls that practically caught themselves. Their sense of anticipation, of luring someone to a better spot, the overhand delivery, the touch on the pass, the subtle nuances of our game that were a joy to behold. They would know their audience clearly. Did you know that all cutters are not created equal? In my world, Brad Kotz, Billy Marino, Vinny Sombrotto and Jon Reese were always open. When my college coach told our team in a huddle my sophomore year "if you see Starsia cutting to his left hand, you do not see him!," I could deal with the truth and the indignity. I can still picture myself refereeing scrimmages at Brown and left to marvel at Darren Lowe's ignoring some open cutters while mining for a better option.

To young players everywhere, whether you are going off to camp, trying to figure out this game or hoping to get recruited at the next level, work on becoming an effective/better passer. There is not a one of those guys in the previous paragraph who would have been a threat in a fastest shot contest. We spend way too much time with that phenomenon and an obsession with it has stunted the growth of many a young player. Learn to pass, learn to pass off the dodge, off the ground, when someone is hanging on your arm. You may find that you have to tighten your pocket some in order to deliver an accurate overhand pass…good! Go ahead, dazzle me with your consistency. We are almost always admonishing young offensive players to throw the ball harder early in their college careers and it is hard to do that with those baggy, low-set pockets. You can shoot it hard at a 6x6 target but, it is a greater challenge to deliver a crisp, accurate pass to a moving target. You will find that you become a better shooter/scorer by becoming a better passer.

I had some wonderful and poignant conversations with "Big Dom" in his late years and will always admire the player who executes a well-thrown pass. Drink plenty of fluids, don't be "too cool for school" and enjoy the 2017 summer season!

*"The true measure of a man is how he treats someone who can do him absolutely no good."*

Ann Landers

## 27

# The Language of Lacrosse

With the start of fall lacrosse, we will all witness the beginning of some new coaching careers. You don't have to be brand new, like Kevin Conry at Michigan, but emerging careers mean the introduction of new philosophies, individual priorities and ultimately, the development of a style and language that will distinguish the delivery of these new unique messages. To this day, after coaching college lacrosse for 42 years, I still only "maybe" would admit to having said the same thing or used the same expression twice over an extended career.

When any group of Brown or Virginia players gather and attempt to mimic things they think they heard coming from me, I am quick to call them out on the exaggeration of those memories. However, there may be some expressions that do resonate with every coach that frame a consistent message over time. You can pick them up from other people, they evolve in your own universe and serve as the pillars of a coaching philosophy. From the recruiting to the end of a final practice, if the message has merit, the method and relationships are strengthened.

When a young man first sits in my office, there is almost always a moment when I will tell him that *"you don't have something till you have something."* Whether it was Virginia or another school, coaches may imply their support hoping you will hang with them. However, you do not have anything concrete until that coach makes a formal offer. Prospects need to keep looking for colleges aggressively until that moment. For the college coaches, my credo for the recruiting was *"make it personal, don't take it personally."* The most significant difference between Carolina and Virginia, between Brown and Penn or Lehigh and Colgate is you!

In any communication with student-athletes, coaches need to be mindful of their language and appreciate that *"you can never take it back."* We are often the most experienced, the most clever, and, potentially, the most sarcastic participants on a practice field. The players give us lots of material. Let me advise you to bite your tongue. They never forget the most acerbic (even if accurate) comments and may use it to sow discontent.

Practice has started, stick drills on the first day and I can hear myself *"throw a ball that catches itself."* It speaks to delivery, pace, situation and location and begins to teach players that they have a greater responsibility than just unloading a pass. I have been blessed with some amazing players and did not want to stifle a creative spirit. However, the oxymoronic theme became *"dazzle me with your consistency."* They needed to understand that the unyielding standard was making the play, at the decisive moment under, perhaps, the most adverse conditions. For most players, that meant the consistent execution of fundamentals. I can still vividly picture the "dazzling" textbook overhand stroke of John Keogh, Darren Lowe, Conor Gill and Kyle Dixon among many others.

I reached out to Casey Powell a month ago to congratulate him on his selection to the Hall of Fame. We both agreed that

From 2004

all this recent talk of playing fast may simply be an attempt to reproduce the magic of a 22-21 game in the Dome in 1997. Virginia and Syracuse have long been exploring the balance between acceleration and execution and one of our principles was always "*be quick, don't rush.*" When the play was flying around, I was always exhorting middies to "*hunt the ball*" in the clearing game. There may be a number of logical patterns but keep working to get open until that ball finds its way into the offensive box. In turn, "*never slide up the field from a short to a long*" while riding. Hold on that short stick until you get some help.

Ask any Virginia player in the 24 year period between 1992 and 2016 about the acronym "WTCG" and they will be quick to tell you *"Win The Close Game."* We set aside time in practice almost every day for WTCG. It could be sprints to win the close game, a groundball drill, a timed end-of-the-game scrimmage set, etc. Unwittingly, the daily talk about "winning the close game" gave us confidence about succeeding in those situations beyond simply the late game execution. Our players never talked about any other possible outcome than winning the close game.

In the larger picture get ready to "*bend your back*" and get to the work required for success. The final drill in every practice the day before a game was groundballs away, to remind us what will likely carry the day in tomorrow's contest. There were "*no big games*" allowed in our world, each required our best effort. I borrowed "*be cool to the pizzer dude*" from Sarah Adams in "This I Believe." That is how Virginia players thought this old Long Islander pronounced Italian pie and it spoke directly to how we want to treat people in our lives, especially those who provide any service.

Finally, the last spoken word on our practice field each day, no matter the circumstance, was "*take care of yourself, take care of each other*" until 9/11/2001 when "*we have a lot to be thankful for*" seemed the right ending. It still is.

*"We must free ourselves of the hope that the sea will ever rest. We must learn to sail in high winds."*

Hamner Grant

*"The moment of victory is much too short to live for that and nothing else."*

Martina Navratilova

*"Though no one can go back and make a brand new start, anyone can start from now and make a brand new ending."*

Carl Bard

*"What you're doing speaks so loudly that I can't hear what you're saying."*

Ralph Waldo Emerson

*"What was seared into him was a deeper sense that we have an obligation to things that are greater than our own self-interest. An obligation to think of consequences, all the way through.*

John McCain

# 28

## Zone Defense

There is a lot of talk these days about whether the introduction of a shot clock this fall will result in a proliferation of zone defense. Especially since the 2011 season, when we switched to a zone defense about 2/3 into the regular season and went on to win the National Championship (see the introduction for more insight), I was constantly asked to talk and give clinics about zone defense. There was a sense that switching to a zone was going to be "the secret sauce" and everyone's key to success. I almost always popped that balloon with my opening observation that "if you stink playing man to man, you are likely going to stink playing a zone." Let me walk you through the sequence of events that put us in a zone and why it worked for us in 2011.

We had just been clobbered by a talented, veteran Maryland team on the previous Saturday and were staring at a game with North Carolina on the following weekend. Under the best of circumstances, we were going to have a hard time matching up with the Heels, especially covering their best attackman, Billy Bitter. It was midday on Monday, when our top defenseman, Matt Lovejoy, walked in the office and declared that he "really wanted the Bitter match-up." Which might have been well and good if he hadn't been in a sling with the trainer in tow saying they were on their way to the doctor's office. I told Matt to hold that thought until we knew the extent of his injury. It was Tuesday when the trainer came in to tell us that Matt would require season-ending surgery immediately. I turned to the other coaches and observed "now what do we do about Bitter?" We always practice some zone but had not played one minute of it during the season to date. A couple of priorities helped us to make decisions…we needed something we could put in quickly and we needed something that was not dramatically different from the general principles that we had been emphasizing from the first day, something that made sense to the players. We were now ten games into our season, with half of those against the very best teams in the nation…we were 33 for 38 on EMD/87%, close to #1 in the country. Was there a way to play some variation of our EMD while utilizing the extra man? I decided we would look at it in practice that day. I can tell you frankly that we were awful in the zone on Tues…to the extent that our goalie, Adam Ghitelman, came to me in tears that evening considering our prospects for the weekend. We were, basically, clueless again on Wednesday but showed a glimmer of recognition at the very end of Thursday's practice. A short, light "day before the game" practice on Friday and the coaches gathered in the locker room afterwards to consider "do we have the nerve to do this tomorrow (on national TV…one of only two regular season games on ESPN!)?" We decided to give it a shot. I can recall vividly when Quint Kessenich saw us in the zone and said "Virginia just forfeited any chance they might have had to compete for a championship." We caught Carolina by surprise that day, they rushed some shots, Adam had a good bead on the ball, Bray Malphrus made a key play in OT, Steele Stanwick got the winner and we stole a game that likely propelled us into the NCAA Tournament.

So, for that 2011 National Championship Virginia team, the zone was born of necessity. Its implementation did require some patience through those first few days and a bold decision going into that first game. By the time we got to the NCAA playoffs we were confident and comfortable with the nuances of playing zone defense.

What I came to realize later on and the reason that it might not be the cure-all for everyone is that we had almost the perfect personnel to play zone. In fact, I have no doubt that we likely would not have been as good in the zone if our best defenseman had not been hurt. The keys for us were…an anxiety about who we were at the moment and a willingness to buy in completely to the coaches' suggestion…Matt went out of the line-up but it created a spot for a back-up LSM, Wyatt Melzer, who communicated well and had a good stick…we took Bray Malphrus, a solid but unspectacular LSM and put him in the middle of the zone where his task was to cover the inside player closest to the ball and create mayhem (absolutely suited his Army Ranger personality)…our goalie got hot and was most comfortable handling the 12-16 yd step downs from the high corners that we were giving up (That shot is about a 50% scoring opportunity in the MLL but less than half of that in the college ranks.)… we were able to play our outstanding SSDM, Chris LaPierre, more because we were not asking as much of him physically and our two base defensemen (Harry Prevas and Scott McWilliams) were egoless and took pride in working well together. If your defensive group is a little light, but is willing to talk, moves smartly, anticipate passing lanes and have good sticks and if you have a goalie who can handle the outside shots, you might have a team that would be good in a zone.

It is not practical to go through all the adjustments required for a successful implementation of the zone in this literary setting. I can tell you that our goals were to take away all shots on the crease, pressure the ball behind, ignore all the individual match-ups and two-man pick plays. We put our toughest kid in the crease, rotated through coverage on the back of the crease, had our two short sticks on the high corners and lived with those 12-16 yd step downs. I recall vividly Rob Pannell scoring from 18 yds out in our quarterfinal game with Cornell and immediately telling the defense "don't sweat it, he can have that all day."

I realize that one of the concerns going into the 2018 season and the new shot clock will be teams playing zone defense all the time. I do not believe that will happen, especially for all the reasons outlined above. Some teams just won't be good in a zone and they will find themselves consistently shredded by a good offensive team. You are not going to hide a mediocre goalie in a zone...again, you are going to give up some quality shots that a goalie just has to handle. I think with the dive back in the game, teams will be less inclined to play a popular version of the zone with the short sticks on the low corners. It is going to be a fascinating 2018 season and I am looking forward to seeing the shot clock implemented by fulltime coaches with the time, expertise and talent to consider all the variables.

*"None are so old as those who have outlived enthusiasm."*
Henry David Thoreau

# 2003 National Championship...
# 15th Anniversary in 2018

It is hard not to consider the intensity of Dave Pietramala or Bill Tierney, the scholarly, "IPAD using" temperament of John Tillman or the studied, calming visage of John Danowski, John Desko or Charlie Toomey as a required approach to championship success at the Division I level. The truth is, however, that things are hardly ever quite as well organized as they might appear or as the coaches might like. More often than not, circumstances and luck play as big a role as "best laid plans" in how these frenetic seasons play out. During this 15th anniversary of Virginia's 2003 National Championship, I would like to take you back to some unexpected developments that led to that championship.

2003 was my 10th season at Virginia and we had been to 5 semifinals in the previous 9 years. In every instance, we either did or would have played a team in the Finals that we had played during the regular season. We generally had scouting reports and game plans in place and would have spent most of the week leading to the semifinals in preparation for that first game. There are not a lot of secrets among the top teams and if you were fortunate to win on Saturday, you gathered quickly with your staff to prepare for a

Brett Hughes and Tillman Johnson, May 2003

sickeningly familiar opponent in the most important game of the year. With one day to prepare, the adjustments were not dramatic.

Hopkins (the #1 seed) and Syracuse played in the first semifinal of the weekend. We had beaten Syracuse 16-15 in the Dome earlier in the season and had lost 8-7 to Hopkins at Homewood. We were actually down 6-0 to Hopkins at halftime, hopeful that we might score a goal in the second half and then Matt Ward had a decent shot to tie it right at the very end. In the meantime, we played Maryland in the second semifinal of Championship Weekend and Tillman Johnson stood on his head in our 14-4 win.

What was different for us in 2003 was my daughter Molly's graduation from college on the Wednesday morning before Championship Weekend. Columbia University is the only college that I am aware of that graduates on a mid-week morning. When Molly and I talked, she understood immediately that it was going to be near-impossible for me to get there. My wife Krissy and son Joe headed to New York City and I had a quiet house for a couple of days before leaving for Baltimore. By Wednesday's practice, we had our semifinal game plan in place and I asked the staff to come back to the office that evening. Marc VanArsdale, David Curry and Hannon Wright were happy to oblige and I suggested that we go back and re-examine our approach to both Syracuse and Hopkins, should we be fortunate to play through.

Hopkins had a great regular season and they were an impressive team. Closer examination revealed a team with a dominating first midfield, that really moved the ball and was uniquely unselfish at the offensive end. They were always looking for the extra pass. We decided that evening to try and use that against them. Given an opportunity to face them again, we would put three poles in the midfield and were determined not to slide, even to our short stick defenders. We were going to cut off the outlets and make them finish their dodges. We had never done that during the season and it is hard to imagine we could have made that adjustment in a short weekend.

Thursday evening of Championship Weekend was a banquet that included all four of the teams. Each team would have an undergraduate representative speak for a few minutes for their institution, a tradition since abandoned. Our Hatcher Snead, who did not play one minute that weekend, was the final student speaker and gave the most memorable and inspiring presentation of Memorial Day priorities. We floated out of that room and it was the first indication that this might be our time. It also speaks to how important each person's role is on a team. You just never know when you might be asked to step up and make a difference.

Walking into the stadium for Friday's shootaround is also a vivid memory. The field looked gorgeous from the tunnel, shimmering and virtually untouched. It did not take long, however, to realize there was a serious problem afoot. The turf was wet and thin and tore up while simply standing to have a catch. I remember saying to the NCAA rep that it was virtually unplayable. It seems the Ravens were going to replace the field with sport turf immediately following the weekend and did not put much into its preparation. There was not much we could do at this point and the field deteriorated throughout the weekend. By Monday's final, you were standing in water over your shoes. I did not know whether it would have a greater effect on the offense or the defense.

The key match-up for us going into a possible final game with Hopkins was going to be a short stick on attackman Peter LeSeur. He was an excellent player but our sense was that he dodged to pass and that we were going to take our chances with him shooting on

Tillman. I stood on the opposite sideline during the first half of the Syracuse/Hopkins semifinal and was at the Hopkins offensive end of the field during the final seconds. LeSeur was dodging a Syracuse defenseman and I found myself talking to John Desko under my breath "don't John, don't, don't slide to him," as if John was actually playing. Syracuse slid to LeSeur, he fed the crease and Hopkins scored just before the half. I knew what we were going to do, if we had the chance!

Hopkins went on to beat Syracuse and our convincing win over Maryland set the stage for Sunday's final. We followed through with the decisions we had made earlier in the week, put poles (Trey Whitty, David Burman and Ned Bowen) on midfielders Donegar, Harrison and Boland, left Brett Hughes on attackman Kyle Barrie and put short sticks on Bobby Benson (Nathan Kenny) and the key match-up of the game, Billy Glading on Peter LeSeur. We did not expect much pressure from Bobby off the dodge but held our breath early when it got to Peter.

We never practiced this set up before the game and with poles up the field and short sticks catching up to the play, went off-sides three times in the first quarter. We settled down, got the lead early behind Chris Rotelli's play and AJ Shannon's four goals, Billy managed the match-up on LeSeur and although Tillman wasn't asked to do as much on this day, he owned the weekend overall.

I have always been smart enough to have great assistant coaches, been fortunate to have worked with talented, creative players and blessed to have had a family that understood and loved what I did for a living. In every instance, it took a group effort to manage success and, in this instance, alongside the obvious contributions of Marc Van, Billy, Chris, AJ, Trey, Tillman, etc. stood Hatcher and…Molly.

...with Chris Rotelli, May 2003

Long-time Assistant and close friend Marc VanArsdale

# 30

## "Mickey"

It may be my dark, little secret that I did not grow up fantasizing about playing midfield for Syracuse or Maryland nor about scoring a winning goal at Homewood. My early formative years were spent on Long Island simply assuming that one day I would be roaming centerfield for the New York Yankees. I was 9 years old in 1961 when Mickey Mantle and Roger Maris had their epic home run chase, when we wanted doubleheaders so that the Yanks could win two on that day and when it seemed that the American League All-Stars were all wearing pinstripes. It was only when I finally got to high school and pitchers started throwing real curve balls that I began to doubt my dream (my foot may still be stuck in that bucket). I went off to college as a football recruit and was talked into playing lacrosse by a freshman teammate. I played in the first game I ever saw that year and almost immediately fell in love with this new sport.

When I began coaching, I needed names for different situations that arose on the field. Whether it was a ride or a clear, a defensive situation or an offensive opportunity, I developed a language that was familiar and easily interpreted. One of our recognition calls, for almost as long as I can recall coaching, was a "Mickey." It was an offensive call that asked the players on the field to find the mismatch that favored us. It might be our best middie covered by a short stick, one of our attackman covered by a vulnerable defender, etc. Rather than call out our player or scream his number, to alert the entire stadium, the "Mickey" call gave our guys credit for identifying the situation and putting ourselves in a position to take advantage of it. It was easily a "Mickey" for this coach because it was a nightmare for any pitcher when Mantle came to the plate.

This all came back to me as I have been watching the highlights for Loyola's Pat Spencer after each of these 2019 early season games. This young man is proving to be a "Mickey" for the Hounds as soon as he emerges from the locker room. Imagine being an opposing defensive coordinator trying to manage the match-up problems that Spencer presents. I am not sure there is a single defender in the country who can limit his opportunities. Do we slide to him early and allow him to use his vision and sense of selflessness to engage his teammates? Or, do we take a chance with his scoring ability, which has greatly improved in the past year? The truly great attackmen are both passers and scorers. The fact that Spencer wears Mickey Mantle's #7 and is being coached most closely by (longtime, former assistant) Marc VanArsdale raises this consideration to an almost surreal level.

I will take all this a step further. In any discussion of who is the best player, I always put it into the context of "If you were starting a team, who would you choose first…?" Well, at this particular moment in history, we are waiting for the PLL to announce six of the best teams ever assembled. I am about to suggest that if we were drafting these teams from scratch, I might take Pat Spencer ahead of any other player on the board. His sense of the game, his physicalness, the way he makes his teammates better and how much he has improved throughout his career might be the right building blocks for a franchise. We are watching a very special lacrosse player in the blossom of his career.

# 31

## My Greatest Gift

I arrived at Brown University in the fall of 1970, the first in a large Catholic Italian-Irish family to leave Long Island for college. I was recruited to Brown University to play football and was selected as a co-captain of that freshmen team (in the days when freshmen were required to play on first-year teams). My high school, Valley Stream Central, did not have lacrosse, even though powerhouse programs at Elmont, Lynbrook and Sewanhaka surrounded us.

Hard as it may be to imagine, I simply had never seen lacrosse before arriving in Providence, RI. A buddy on the football team talked me into playing that spring of 1971 and I fell in love with everything about the game from that first day. I also quickly decided that I wanted to be known for being more than just a good athlete and worked relentlessly on improving my stick work. My trick question to young campers is whether it is allowed to work outside on the wall if it happens to be raining or snowing. I don't think I missed a day after first picking up a stick that spring.

I tried out for the US National Team in 1977, and you can imagine my joy upon receiving the letter announcing my selection to the team. To this day, it sits near the top of a very short list of my most memorable athletic achievements. I was in great shape and very excited as we moved toward the start of those 1978 games in Stockport, England. I was so proud to be part of a US Team that had never lost a game in international play.

We swept the field in the preliminary rounds and faced a Canadian team in the championship game that we had previously beaten 28-4. That score was more of an aberration than any other. This was a Canadian team that included David Huntley, Mike French, Stan Cockerton, Jim Calder, John Grant Sr. and North Carolina State's goalie, Bob Flintoff.

We were down 8-4 at the end of the first quarter in that championship game, and had fought back to put ourselves up two with about three minutes to play. I knocked a ball down in our defensive end, picked it up and headed up the field. If I had pulled it out and just thrown it to Eamon McEneaney or Tom Postel, we likely would have buried the game right there. Instead, in my haste, the defense froze, I charged down the middle of the field and clanged the ball off the crossbar. The rebound found its way to the midfield line. A Canadian attackman picked it up and scored. Canada won the ensuing faceoff, scored again and then won the game on an extra-man goal in overtime. It was devastating to have my most glorious achievement distinguished by a mental mistake that may have cost us the game and the championship.

While the result was a harbinger of things to come with regard to Canada's potential in the field game, the residual effect was one of the great lessons for a young coach. There are times when we feel like these young players are not listening to us. Why don't they do what we ask, what we have them do in practice? Why are they trying to hurt me? It actually feels personal.

When I have those thoughts, I remember back to a young defenseman who worked so hard to get it right and was still capable of a mental error at the most inopportune time. That mistake turned out to be one of my greatest gifts to all the young men I have coached during these past 42 years. It taught me patience, possibly the most important quality for coaches at all levels.

It still hurts but I became a better coach for the experience.

1978 USA Team

*"I've got things to do with my life."*

Pat Tillman

*"Character may be manifested in the great moments, but it is made in the small ones."*

Phillip Brooks

*"Victory awaits him who has everything in order—LUCK people call it. Defeat is certain for him who has neglected to take the necessary precautions in time; this is called bad luck."*

Roald Amundsen

*"The truth is that most people have a better chance to be uncommon by effort than by natural gifts."*

Tony Dungy

LIFE

# 32

# Why We Play

Between thinking about the agony that accompanied the ending of Coach Tony Bennett's 2017-18 UVA basketball season (the first time in history a #1 seed lost to a #16 in the first round) and spending a day with Mikey Thompson and the Christopher Newport team recently, it brought to mind a theme I have addressed in multiple settings. If I had to boil down to a sentence what it has been that I have been doing these past 42 years, it would be having tried every method to convince young men that "it is worth it" to make the commitment and sacrifices required for success. There will not be a lot of other occasions in their lives when they can experience the satisfaction that accompanies a group pulling together to reach their potential. I always found hope in a reading from a variation of Philippians 2:2 that "there is no joy the world can give like that which comes from joining good men in common purpose."

If that rings true, it speaks directly to the question of why we play team sports and the value of that participation. The experience begins with the first rough housing at home with family and friends. An indelible impression accompanies our first exposure to coaching and influences a willingness or an aversion to our athletic future. A joyful coach, a respected mentor can have a profound effect on the future of young athletes. It is also in these very early experiences that we begin to learn to compete. I am not going to apologize for recognizing the value of competition. I realize there is a movement afoot to encourage the "everyone gets a trophy" mentality but, ultimately, it misses the point. While there is a physical value to participation in sports and a fellowship and sportsmanship component, there is also a reaction to the competition piece that will begin to define an evolving personality.

As many times as I had Scott Smith officiating pivotal Virginia Lacrosse games during my years in Charlottesville, that is how many times I told Scott that my favorite coaching book was the one authored by his father, Dean, the Hall of Fame basketball coach at UNC. I may have been trying to get into Scott's good graces in every instance but early in *A Coach's Life* his father wrote about "the value in exploring the athletic heart on the championship level." What a beautifully simple yet profound explanation for the athletic experience.

There are two important components to consider here. The first involves the actual competition, especially as it applies to players and coaches. When I am teaching stickwork to young players, I am always talking about being able to make a play at that moment when the outcome of a game is actually being decided. You can win a wall ball competition, you can do line drills efficiently, you can play well, you can adjust to the natural ebb and flow of a game for the first three quarters…do you step center stage late in a game?, can you make that same play when you are tired, when you are hurt, when your teammates are looking around, when you can ignore whether or not you will be the hero and simply focus on the task? This is a very real phenomenon and one that every athlete considers when he steps onto the field. What do we find out about ourselves during the actual competition?

The second, possibly even more important, component is your reaction to the outcome of each contest. If everyone is going home with a trophy, it subtly softens the relative anguish of a loss. It is learning to deal with the winning and losing that may be the most valuable lessons learned from athletic competition. Michael Jordan talks all the time about the shots he did not make at the end of games and being cut from his high school basketball team. We (players, coaches and fans) learn from both the winning and the losing but the most profound messages accompany our reaction to the games we do not win. It is "easy" to process winning and the self-examination of performance is not nearly as thorough and severe as it would be following a less desirable outcome. This applies to everyone associated with the competition, parents and fans alike. Every game we play, from lunchtime hoops and HORSE in the backyard, pick-up six a side soccer, a chess tournament, summer league lacrosse games, wiffle ball in the driveway, etc. provides us with opportunities to learn how to deal with results.

Participation in the athletic arena is NOT a zero sum activity, although it often can feel thus. Peter Lasagna recently reminded me how often I would talk about how the feeling after a one-goal game was so disproportionate to how the game may have actually unfolded. In the 2004 National Championship game, Syracuse did "win" but no one who witnessed the contest would deny that the Midshipmen were "winners" that day. The results are certainly an obvious factor but it is the relationships, the effort, the execution and the reaction that should carry and define the day.

I have often said that there is no deserve in sports, at times the outcomes of these games seem so unfair and arbitrary. While championships, jobs, bonuses, roster spots, etc. are often being determined by these outcomes, it is beside the point when considering the essence of competition. There is an old saying "life is 10% what happens to you and 90% how you respond to it." We keep score because learning to win with grace and lose with dignity affects every part of our lives. We need to experience both of those outcomes on an unexceptional basis in order to develop a balanced and reflective personality. As parents, coaches, fans, participants and, most importantly, as mentors to those over whom we have influence, one of our most profound responsibilities is teaching the value of both circumstances.

Play, enjoy, compete and process the results for their prudent value.

# 33

## For the Good of the Game

This past summer, Mike Murphy, the head coach at UPenn and Vice President of the college coaches' association (IMLCA), asked me to chair a new "Champion The Game" committee as part of the association's strategic plan initiative. Well, I have spent a lot of time on the road these past few months and have spent a lot of time thinking about our game. How do we improve college lacrosse? How do we grow the game and re-energize Championship Weekend? Most importantly, how do we strengthen our position as role models for the next generation and as good stewards of the game we have all come to love. Some of these ideas are simply my affirmation for topics that have been endlessly debated and some are new and clearly require greater consideration. The NCAA Rules Committee can only recommend changes every two years and 2017 is a "rule change summer." Whatever the committee chooses to or chooses not to act on will be in place until 2019. Here goes…

• Mandate a 60 second shot clock when the ball crosses the midline…what other sport asks the officials to interpret the intentions of a player or a pattern of play? Every referee calls this differently and EVERY game is officiated differently in the last five minutes, as dictated by the scoreboard. Coaches are screaming at the officials, the fans have no idea what is going on and human nature demands that the team with the lead gets a quicker clock. The MLL players love their game and I watched a terrific women's game recently between Maryland and Virginia. The women have greatly improved their game and the clocks are now sitting there available at every institution. It just makes too much sense, let's try it for two years.

• NCAA proposal that would prohibit any off-campus lacrosse evaluations from September 1st until the date of the NCAA Finals. Coaches need to be accessible to their players and their families during the school year and this would encourage multi-sport HS participation. Prospect days are allowed but you can only work your own.

• Emphasize the Native American roots of the game, especially during Championship Weekend. I addressed this in another article and this would require support from the NCAA Lacrosse Committee. I would strongly suggest that the NCAA Committee explore a relationship with the Native American community that honors the roots of the sport and elevates those graceful traditions.

• Make the overtime periods in a game 15 minutes long with each coach having one TO per period. Why are they presently four minutes long with both coaches getting use of a time-out in each one?…time-outs that the coaches almost always use. It computes to almost 8 time-outs available for a single 15 minute period. When Virginia and Maryland played a seven OT period game, both Dave Cottle and myself used every TO available through the first six periods (24 minutes of lacrosse, 12 TO's).

Brian Carroll scored the winner in the 7th OT when we did not use our available TO. (RC)

• It will be very difficult for the NCAA or for the individual institutions to agree to extend the regular season into the late spring. It is simply too complicated and too expensive. I realize that popular sentiment is to start the season later but there is too much good lacrosse happening in February to take that scheduling flexibility away from the programs. Virginia has played at Loyola in two of the last three years on the first Saturday of February. It has been Loyola's best-attended game of the year both times...get a warm coat. My suggestion would be an NCAA proposal that prohibits any games or scrimmages before February 1st and twenty-hour practice weeks cannot begin any earlier than two weeks before your first competition (game or scrimmage).

• Sit down for this one coaches...an NCAA proposal that would limit coaches to only two hours in any University athletic facility during one day of your designated seven-day practice week. How could you possibly monitor this? You might be surprised how diligent coaches are about following NCAA rules. Do you want the players to actually have a day off? Keep the coaches out of the office.

• Use retired coaches as hosts during Championship Weekend. We have talked about hosting Athletic Directors and dignitaries from emerging institutions at our premier event but the most influential coaches are too busy to attend to this during the season and too tired at the end. The IMLCA should arrange for a box during the Weekend and cover the expenses for Richie Moran, Roy Simmons, Jack Emmer, Sid Jamison, Carl Runk,

Ray Rostan, etc. to plan for the weekend, communicate with targeted officials and host them on game day. Retired coaches are a valuable resource we could put to better use. Who wouldn't be sold on lacrosse after spending most of a day with Richie Moran?!

- These last two go together. It may not be realistic to extend the regular season but I would like us to consider splitting up Championship Weekend. Before we do that, though, I believe we should approach the women about combining the men's and women's championships. I think we could create a gala event unlike anything that currently happens in NCAA sports. It would speak to the "specialness" of our game and the willingness of ALL participants to work together. Our Championship has diminished some in recent years and the women's event has slowly grown. Let's meet in the middle and take advantage of combining our resources (both separate events scheduled for the same weekend in Foxboro this May). Here's how it would work…Memorial Day Weekend—women's DI semifinals on Friday night (same as now), men's DI semifinals on Saturday night (same)…either put one game on Saturday before the semis or play all four M & W DII/DIII Championship Games on Sunday. We would need a sport turf surface and I would recommend a University site. This would still be a great weekend of lacrosse for a family travelling a distance and folks could travel home in a reasonable manner on the holiday.

The Men's and Women's DI Championship Games would be played on the following Saturday. ESPN has requested that the Men's Championship Game be played in primetime on Memorial Day Monday. I have always respected that the committee decided that was too great a burden for families travelling to the weekend.

With this new split set-up, we might have our game highlighted in prime time in one of these new, large metropolitan area soccer stadiums (20-25K would seem the right size and a grass surface could accommodate back-to-back men's and women's games). In addition, the week between semifinals and finals gives the players a chance to recover and the coaches a chance to prepare. Have you ever noticed that the best lacrosse of the Final Four weekend generally happens in the semifinals? It is really hard to turn around in less than 48 hours on the hottest weekend of the year to play in the most important game (of your life). With a week in between the games, played in (possibly) prime time, we are likely to have our two best teams playing their best.

One man's opinion…thanks!

# 34

# The Rules Committee

I served on the NCAA Men's Lacrosse Committee for five years, beginning in 1997. One of the first indications that my professional life had now changed came in the form of correspondence from a fan who found me a "despicable lacrosse elitist" to have excluded an undefeated Bucknell team from the tournament in 1996. I wasn't even on the committee for the Bucknell decision, which did not seem to diminish this fan's passion for tournament selections and/or rule changes for lacrosse. Until about ten years ago, the men's committee was a more equitable composition between coaches and administrators and handled both the selection of the teams for the NCAA Tournament and all rule changes. Those tasks are now handled by two separate groups—the Tournament Selection Committee and the Rules Committee. It is the Rules Committee that is meeting this week in Indianapolis to consider a shot clock, restoring the dive, etc. and any new changes will be in effect for two years.

I still have a very vivid recollection of that initial year on the committee and feeling that it was the first adult thing I had been required to do as a college lacrosse coach. Picking the teams for the tournament may have been a challenge but it paled in comparison to facing my coaching peers of the teams that had not been selected. You were buried in meeting rooms for 3-4 days with people you respected and who were trying to do the right thing. There was a tendency to lose track of having to pop your head out and finding that everyone did not agree with those tough decisions. It did not take long to anticipate the spirited criticism that accompanied the selection of the tournament field, no matter who was selected.

There is no doubt that this 2018 committee will be having a similar discussion to the one that our committee debated long and hard in 2000. Bryan Matthews, then the athletic director at Washington College, opened the rules component of our meeting with an impassioned recommendation that our sport needed a shot clock. We talked about little else over the next 24-36 hours. I was generally an advocate of the idea but knew it would be received with mixed feelings by the coaches overall and was not sure what I would do if it came down to a vote. Well, it did come down to a vote and Virginia came up last on the alphabetical tally. I did not know what I was going to do as the voting started but John Desko's vote immediately before mine confirmed the issue. I did not want John to be hung out as the sole deciding vote and was happy to support him with an affirmative vote to approve the clock.

The decision to approve the shot clock in 2000 may have caught the coaching community by surprise and those who disagreed with the decision drowned out any thoughtful discussion of its implementation. The committee withdrew its recommendation that fall and variations of "speeding up the game" have brought us to this point in 2018. I still think our game would benefit from a shot clock…the unintentional yet inevitable inconsistencies of officiating personalities, the wasted game time of changing personnel on the fly, putting more of a premium on two-way midfielders, etc. I do not believe we would necessarily see a proliferation of zone defenses, we can try it without a two point shot, there would be an immediate increased interest in taking advantage of transition and early offensive opportunities and it is not going to take coaching out of the game (which, if it did happen, might actually be a positive development). As a matter of fact, I think it would be very exciting to see our best and brightest coaches preparing their teams to implement the shot clock.

To the 2018 Rules Committee…you are going to get some grief either way, do what you think is right for the game!

# 35

## The Virginia/Maryland Rivalry

When asked to put together some thoughts about the Virginia/Maryland rivalry during the past quarter century, I almost immediately began to get the shakes. My experience with the Terps pre-dates my arrival in Charlottesville in the fall of 1992. The first time was as a player in a 1973 NCAA playoff game against Frank Urso, Doug Schreiber, Mike Thearle and, simply, one of the finest college teams in our sport's history. The last time at Brown was when the Terps came to Providence and beat our undefeated 1991 team in the NCAA Quarterfinals behind Steve Kavovit's playoff record 31 saves. Dick Edell and I had a good laugh during one of my final visits to his home as he recalled the Brown fans hanging over the railing almost in their huddles.

I had heard talk about the difference in the play of ACC games, about the ferocity of the competition that accompanied the familiarity among all the participants. I was given a very non-collegial introduction to Virginia/Maryland in my first season and quickly came to understand and appreciate the rivalry. We played 38 times in the 21 years between my arrival in 1993 and 2014, Maryland's final year as a member of the Conference. We played three times in 2008, splitting the first two and then winning in OT in the NCAA quarterfinals behind Ben Rubeor.

Thirteen of those games were decided by one goal, including my first two in 1993. We had beaten them in OT in the regular season and then had to play them again in the ACC Tournament semifinals. Late in that game, we were struggling to clear the ball and I called a timeout with the ball still in our defensive end. Within the first five seconds of the whistle to re-start the play, we immediately went offsides...as if that was what we had diagrammed in our huddle. I turned to Assistant Coach Marc VanArsdale and whispered that "I could get fired over that"! We went on to lose in OT.

We stormed the field in the 1997 regular season before the referees could reconsider and won 15-14 in the second OT on a collision play around the goal by Drew McKnight. I was on the NCAA committee that year and will take some of the credit (blame?) for getting the Terps into the tournament at all that year. They were a lot better than their record in '97 and returned the favor by beating us in the NCAA Quarterfinals in College Park 10-9.

Our first National Championship team took a beating on the road at Hopkins in 1999. We were in and out with our goalies throughout the game and unsettled at the defensive end. In our very next game, our freshman goalie Derek Kenny played very well in a 13-4 win over the Terps that gave us a renewed sense of confidence as we moved toward the playoffs. In 2003, it was another tale of the goalies. The Terps beat us 8-7 in the regular season and we faced them again in the semifinals in Ravens Stadium. In a performance for the ages, Tillman Johnson dismissed the muddy conditions and stood on his head in a convincing win.

Coach Cottle bought his Terps to Charlottesville in 2009 for a game that had all the markings of another close-fought, intense contest. However, no one was quite prepared for a game

Krissy and Molly at Klockner Stadium

that set an NCAA record and took seven OTs to decide. Each of the coaches had utilized all their timeouts during the first six overtimes and after we had regained possession in the seventh, I decided to let it go. Frankly, I had run out of things to say anyway and Brian Carroll immediately hit a shot on the run, making the coaches seem smarter than they deserved.

It was only a few years from the end of this rivalry when the two teams finally met in a National Championship game. We had fully expected to face the Terps for a third time in the final game of 2006 but UMass changed that script. We limped into the playoffs in 2011, had lost our best defenseman, Matt Lovejoy, for the season in a smack-down by Maryland at Scott Stadium that had defined our regular season struggles. We switched over to a zone defense shortly thereafter and were still a little undecided on our approach in the championship game. On Maryland's very first possession, Grant Catalino streaked across the middle and gave them the early lead. That was all we needed to see; we settled back into the zone and won the National Championship 9-7.

I will forever remember the ferocious competition and memorable results that accompanied the Virginia/Maryland rivalry. Any number of those games epitomized the very best of college lacrosse. At the same time, the rivalry will forever be defined in my heart by how quickly Coach Edell and I could put those results behind us when we met on the field afterwards. I have such a vivid memory of both our families gathered together at Klockner. I might never have considered that it was possible to have a soft spot for the Terps but, there it is…Maryland/Virginia, it's good for the game!

# 36

# The Elephant In The Room

I have often been asked, "what is the toughest part of coaching college lacrosse?" The obvious response would most likely fall somewhere on the spectrum of…the recruiting, generating offense against Notre Dame, dealing with Syracuse's athleticism, Denver's deliberate pace of play, the recent streak of futility against Duke, etc. I would have to say that it is none of those things. I don't think I would stand alone when I suggest that the most frustrating challenge for college lacrosse coaches is dealing with the irresponsible use of alcohol by college undergraduates. Drug use in college is not as pervasive an issue with Division I players because of the random drug testing at most institutions. It clearly happens but the testing is a deterrent. It is the misuse of alcohol that overwhelms student-athlete behavior.

I had two recent conversations that engaged this topic in an interconnected way. The first was a wonderful talk with Brian Holman, who was so genuinely excited about the opportunity for our sport that was unfolding in Utah. People talk about Utah as the "Gateway to the West" for men's lacrosse and Brian is awash with the potential for that development. What a transcendent moment! The other was with a college classmate, Don Bogan, who is a faculty member at the University of Oklahoma School of Law. Knowing that he had some connections to the lacrosse world, a couple of colleagues had asked him about the possible growth of the game in Oklahoma and the reality of "the reputation that lacrosse players had developed for being lawless, rowdy, over-the-top, cliquish miscreants." I am sure the question had to do with the national publicity that accompanied the recent events at Duke and Virginia. The argument that "nothing" really happened at Duke and that Virginia may have been an isolated tragedy dismisses the common thread in both instances. Look outside the ACC to the very recent fraternity event at Penn State, to the trials still going on at Vanderbilt and to the recent conviction of a Stanford swimmer. These are all great schools, good students and most with high-end athletic aspirations. I hardly say "always or never" to my athletes but it is close to the truth to suggest that EVERY unfortunate incident on a college campus begins with the irresponsible use of alcohol. I also believe that the data is there to confirm that it is worse in men's lacrosse than most sports. If I am an administrator considering adding men's lacrosse to my institutional community, I am thinking long and hard about that boorish reputation. How do we enhance the growth of the game and, never mind the reputation, how do we change the data?

Everyone has a responsibility here. College coaches need to elevate their role as educators and address this topic directly and consistently. Players are now committed for two full years before they arrive on campus. Coaches can use this time to be very explicit with these recruits about expectations for their behavior during their last two high school years and to send a very clear, frank message about their behavior during a recruiting visit, orientation and, finally, their arrival on campus to begin their matriculation. You might consider forming social "pods" within the team. Pick 6-8 older leaders, have them draft the entire roster onto their individual pods and then, have them be responsible for everyone within their group. If someone is irresponsible, the entire pod bears the consequence. You will find the players putting pressure on each other to toe the line. Coaches need to be role models and never consume alcohol in the company of undergraduates and parents. Every personal signal needs to be clear and uncompromising.

The parents have a very important role here. Before each season the parents need to meet and confirm that they will NEVER provide alcohol for a college undergraduate. I am challenging all parents to help the coaches and your son's team to meet their potential. Drinking with your child can wait until after graduation. Parents who provide alcohol to players in post-game situations are legitimizing their son's participation in the late night behavior that follows. You do not have to have been a college coach for 42 years to fully appreciate how challenging parents can make the job in this important area. "I really want to help my son's team, what can I do?"...this is what you can do!

Finally, to the players, you are in college, you are starting to form into the person you are going to be, beginning to identify your life's priorities...What Are You Willing To Do? Don't insult me...irresponsible use of alcohol diminishes individual performance in the classroom and on the field, there are almost as many injuries on the late night corner as on the practice field, it can interfere with relationships among teammates, and any suspended players hurt the team's overall effort. When we first truly addressed this issue at UVA in 1999, I sent that very question to the players over Thanksgiving. One of the players wrote back that "if you could promise me that we would win the National Championship, I would be willing to give up alcohol." That's not how it works son, first you make the commitment and acknowledge the sacrifice and then, maybe, the success will follow. What I can assure you is that this leap of faith is worth whatever sacrifices are required. All the parties, all the silliness will blend in one to the other, you will hardly recall a moment. However, if you beat Hopkins, make the playoffs, play closer than you ever have to your team's potential, you will be talking about it at your 25th reunion as if it happened yesterday.

I tell young players all the time that, if treated respectfully, lacrosse can be your friend for a long time. There are many of us still involved in the game who comfortably recall a respectful, yet irreverent, social club behavior that surrounded the game even at the highest level. Everyone seems to agree that the game is at a crossroads, perhaps about to explode upon the national scene. I put it to the players...it is time for the game to grow-up off the field. Administrators will hand you a copy of the laws/rules, the coaches will work hard to encourage appropriate behavior, I cannot speak for the parents but, no matter...it needs to come from you. These things don't work pushed down from above, the change needs to bubble up from within. It should feel hard in the beginning, it will be the mountain of anticipation that seems so daunting. It will be worth it, however, and I encourage you to seize this moment. Be forever known as the generation that changed the legacy of our game.

# 37

# Highlights

When I visited High Point College in the Spring of 2017, one of the players asked me about the highlights of my career. I will return to my specific response to his question later on but, it gave me a moment to step back and consider some of the things that I have seen in these past 47 years of college lacrosse, especially those that I instantly appreciated having been blessed to have been a part of or witness to directly...here are some of those:

• The poise that John Danowski demonstrated in 2013 on the field following his team's National Championship win over Syracuse. You can only begin to imagine the bedlam going on around the head coach and for John to ask his team to remove the NCAA Championship t-shirts before going through the handshake line with the Orange, very impressive...

• The Cornell teams of the late 70s are still my favorite

• Did Leonard Bernstein have a sweeter set of hands than Jeff Long, Navy '77?

• Jack McGetrick's passion for life and lacrosse and his generous spirit and patience with a young, raw defenseman back in the summer of '71 and '72, when he was a 1ˢᵗ Team AA Defenseman from Cortland.

● The hardest checkers were Mike Thearle, Maryland '73 and Bruce Roundpoint, Akwesasne. Cross the middle of the floor at your own risk…

● The most explosive set of hands I have ever seen belonged to goalie Sal Locasio. Sal was the NE Player of the Year all four years while at UMass, '85-'89.

● Two of the fastest players I have ever seen still to this day played against each other in the spring of 1979 in Lexington, VA. Mark Farnham from Brown started chasing Jeff Fritz from W & L around that field and every other participant and fan was treated to two members of a very exclusive club…everyone else may as well have waved at them as they went by!

● Have any middies moved off the ball as smartly as Vin Sombrotto, LIAC, Billy Marino, Cornell '76 and Brad Kotz, Syracuse '85?

● One of the most raw athletes and yet, dynamic and effective offensive players was John Fay, New Hampshire '81. John could actually shoot it with one hand on the run from the midfield and it was a sound play and a legit scoring threat.

● Has a middie ever had a better season than Yale's Jon Reese did in 1990 scoring 82 & 15? He had 10 goals one day and 8 a couple of days later against solid Army and UMass teams and did not really dodge. I was the head coach of the North-South Game that year and my first midfield was Gait, Gait and Reese!

• Favorite attack unit of all-time…here are my top three—Cornell's MacEnaney, French and Levine, Princeton's Hess, Massey and Hubbard and UVA's Knight, Whiteley and Watson… you decide.

• The greatest sequence of lacrosse (and one of the great individual performances) happened in the Dome in 1997. A play that started with Drew Melchionni picking up a tough GB in Virginia's defensive end, ended with Casey Powell sticking one on the dead run, behind his back, with Chris Sanderson in the goal. It happened in the 4th quarter of the 22-21 Virginia/Syracuse classic. I believe Casey finished 7 & 5.

• It was early 1993, my first spring at Virginia and, in the snow, Roanoke was playing Salisbury on the astroturf at Scott Stadium at 11:00am on a weekday morning. There was a short, stocky attackman from Salisbury who had ten goals that day in his first college contest. Tough as nails and couldn't miss…Jason Coffman broke every national scoring record and went on to the most decorated career in college lacrosse history.

• One of the greatest hits on a lacrosse field happened during a Brown/Penn game at Franklin Field in 1988. Chris Flynn from Penn and Walt Cataldo from Brown were the Offensive and Defensive Players of the Year in FOOTBALL from that fall with a long history of facing each other in FB and Lax. There was a GB at the midline area and I happened to look up and saw that they each had a bead on the play. I remember distinctly thinking to myself, "Oh, please, no" and a collision ensued that had little to do with the play, the ball, or the rest of humanity. They both staggered off…I have no memory of what happened to the ball.

• Before there were radar guns, the fastest shots I ever saw belonged to Ron Fraser, SU '65, Travis Cook, LesCaribous '75 and Greg Tarbell, SU '82

• Having the opportunity to watch Darren Lowe, Brown '92 influence cutters and deliver catchable balls to his teammates was a daily practice perk.

• Tufts getting back to the D3 Finals the year after having won their first championship in 2010. It is hard to go back to back and Tufts getting there the year after was the clearest signal that there was something special afoot in Medford, Mass.

• I was tapped on the shoulder at the 2016 IMLCA Hall of Fame induction and turned to see a modest-sized, long haired gentleman with his hand extended. He said "Coach Starsia, my name is Jimmy Lewis and I have heard you wanted to meet me." The player I wish I had seen and possibly the greatest of all-time, what an honor. Did you know that he had never played soccer before arriving at Navy in the fall of 1961 and went on to score the winning goal in the National Championship game four years later?

• Virginia scrimmaged the Toyota Lacrosse Club while awaiting the start of the playoffs in 1998. Gary Gait was playing for Toyota and while carrying the ball up top, our munchkins on the bench started hollering "he's all left, he's all left." Without hesitation, Gary split to his right and stuck one from 16 yards over our goalie's shoulder. He was so cool, he never even looked over at us as he jogged slowly to the bench. I was smiling.

- I would choose the 1994 NCAA Semifinal over that '97 game in the Dome as the greatest I have ever been a part of, probably because of the setting and final result. We were down 5 goals and two-men down to start the fourth quarter as the #5 seed playing the #1 Orange. That we came back and won in the second overtime was the beginning of a magical streak of games between Virginia and Syracuse and catapulted UVA into the national consciousness.

- The only player I went out of my way to find his game by game highlights on Sunday was Lyle Thompson at Albany. My goodness, what a player, we have all been blessed.

- My response to the High Point player was that "alongside any championships and awards that may have come my way during a long career, one of the true highlights was joining Zed Williams and his family for his graduation from UVA in the Spring of 2017." In all my years, no one had travelled a greater distance from commitment to college graduate. I asked one of his brothers if it was ever hard to get him to go back to school after returning home and his simple reply was "every time." Losing his dad midway through his final spring made the whole saga even more complicated and emotional for everyone involved. I could not be more proud of a young man that I came to know in these 47 years.

Bernie Buonanno and Walt Cataldo with Molly and Joe, 1988

# 38

## Recruiting...The Second Season

With the conclusion of another exciting college lacrosse season, coaches' attention now turns to a time of the year that defines the measure of success for a program in a manner that is only slightly less vital than the spring season itself...recruiting. I have always found it endlessly amusing to consider the serious countenance and intent that consumes Mel Kiper, Todd McShay and the other football recruiting experts when I am reminded of the indecision that accompanied the choice between Peyton Manning and Ryan Leaf. How could people who think about this all the time have so miscalculated the distance and direction between the careers of, perhaps, the NFL's greatest QB and its biggest bust? For all the money, resources and manpower invested in these personnel decisions, it is still hardly an exact science and the best decisions were more likely determined by someone's gut instinct.

A major component of whatever success I may have attained over a long career goes back to a realization I came to during my early years at Brown. Two things—I was smart enough to appreciate quickly that I was a better coach when I had good players. Second, I was going to have to spend so much time recruiting that I had to learn how to sincerely enjoy the process. Having been blessed to have worked at two good schools, I encountered lots of quality candidates from good families. I tried to make the process unique, different and personal in each situation. At the same time, there were enough instances where instinct trumped logic and reason.

I was dating Bates head coach Peter Lasagna's sister when I met him for the first time in the fall of 1976. Peter's family had moved from Baltimore to Rochester just as he was approaching high school. His reputation as an exuberant Mt Washington Mosquito never manifested itself during his HS years in New York. Meanwhile, I was still an assistant coach at Brown in charge of all the recruiting. When I presented the candidates to head coach Cliff Stevenson, his only comment regarding Peter's modest HS credentials was "you must really like her." Thus, a hall of fame coaching and writing career was born and, oh…I married his sister.

The most important recruit in all my years was a high school All-American (when that meant something) attackman from Manhasset HS, John Keogh. It was announced that I would be the head coach at Brown in 1981, a year before taking over the program. In turn, my first recruiting class was already on campus in my first year. John took a chance on a young head coach in the years when the best south shore LI guys were more likely headed to Cornell and the north shore ones to Princeton. Darren Muller, Chris Abbott, Scott Lohan and Vin DiPalma all followed John to Providence and my career got off to a great start. John is currently the COO of CHUBB and we still talk regularly.

David Evans was in my final recruiting class at Brown and an understanding admissions person's comment, "he better be good," prefaced a solid undergraduate career in the classroom and an All-American performance on the field.

First team AA middie and 2011 NCAA Tournament MVP Colin Brigg's career began with a ten second piece of videotape. I had never heard of Colin until viewing that one split dodge and I immediately called into Coach VanArsdale to say "you need to look at this." We both agreed and offered Colin a spot.

I am not sure that I ever actually saw Pat Buchanan, UVA '06, play before hearing that he was a starting OLB on his HS football team and the state of Virginia high hurdle champion. Did I really need to see him play? Pat's brother, Peter, officiated this most recent NCAA D1 championship game.

I took my son Joe with me and had a warm home visit with Mike Powell and his family. I was encouraged when Mike told me that he "wanted to go to school in the south." He remained a man of his word, Syracuse is south of Carthage, NY.

Before it was popular, five Canadians arrived in Providence in the fall of 1983, my second class.

You may be aware that I inadvertently saw future Hall of Famer Doug Knight in my final spring as the head coach at Brown. I was at Westminister School to see another player when this unorthodox, fearless player kept popping into view. Doug's plans were more likely soccer and hockey at a Division 3 school when I talked him into coming to Virginia to play lacrosse. His storied college career included him hosting another future Hall of Famer, Jesse Hubbard, on his official visit. When Doug called me on the Sunday morning of Jesse's visit to inform me that he had no idea where Jesse was at that moment, I wasn't certain that Doug would make it to the start of his second year. When we finally located Jesse at a diner casually visiting with some friends, he may have been confirming his plans to go to Princeton.

I had one spot left in the Virginia class of 2006 and was undecided between Matt Poskay, an unorthodox player from New Jersey who held the national goal scoring record and, JJ

Morrissey, an undersized middie from Massachusetts I had never seen play. Matt Played for a B conference school and had scored 500 goals without dodging or even carrying the ball. JJ came up and introduced himself at a camp that I could not stay at long enough to watch him play. He stuck out his hand, looked me in the eye, working a little Fu Manchu in high school and absolutely bowlegged. He was very engaging and I turned to my wife and mentioned "boy, I hope we recruit that kid." JJ's summer lacrosse was over and he had no video from the previous spring. When it came down to it, we offered the final spot in the class to the guy who scored all the goals. JJ was very gracious and I assumed he would head to a D3 school in NE. When he came back to me a couple of weeks later to ask if there was anything I could do, I called in a marker or two and found a spot. The two last guys in that 2006 class graduated with two national championship rings, Matt a 2xAA and JJ the captain of that undefeated team.

Finally, the first Harlem Lacrosse graduate to earn a full athletic scholarship is a young man by the name of D'Jae Pearson. His recruiting journey to Bryant College began in the most unassuming way. I was sitting with Mike Pressler at Chris Rotelli's camp in San Francisco in the summer of 2017. When I casually asked Mike if he had completed his recruiting for the Class of 2018, he replied "basically, yes, I have one spot but no scholarship." When his reply to what position he was looking for was "LSM," I told "I got him." Knowing that I was no longer actively involved in the recruiting, his "what do you mean, you got him?" was a reasonable reaction. I told him about a young man in New York City who was, perhaps, the best football player on the top high school football program in the City and who was an emerging lacrosse star. D'Jae had just graduated from Frederick Douglas

Academy on 148th St in Harlem and was on his way to a PG year at Blair Academy. Mike immediately called the HS coach to confirm some academic numbers and then called someone at Bryant to arrange for a visit. We left the camp on Monday, D'Jae was on the Bryant campus that Thursday. When Mike called to say that D'Jae was admissible and would earn almost half in merit scholarships, he was excited about the possibility. I am sure he was disappointed to have me say "that's great Mike but he can't come for a half, he has no means at all." We went round and round for a couple of weeks until someone suggested to take D'Jae's highlight video to the football coach, who immediately agreed to fill in the rest of the scholarship package. The rest may be history... keep your eye out for D'Jae Pearson on the football and lacrosse fields at Bryant College come the start of the 2018-19 school year.

John Keogh, Chris Esemplare and Tom Gagnon with Molly, 1985

With Dave White and Steph Russo, Ft. Lauderdale, January '17

# 39

# The Lighter Side of Lacrosse

One of the lessons I consistently communicated to my teams was that it was OK to smile during practice, you were allowed and encouraged to enjoy yourself. As a matter of fact and principle, you are more likely to have an open mind with a smile on your face, ready for new ideas, eager to learn. With the growth of the game, mounting financial commitments and the unrelenting presence of social media, it has become increasingly difficult to maintain a sense of the irony and the humor that may actually enhance success. I am blessed to have had moments during a long career that kept me sane and grounded, able to get through another day. Let me share a couple...

• I played in the first lacrosse game I ever saw as a freshman at Brown in the spring of 1971. The following 1972 summer, I visited with a Native American teammate and close friend, David White, at his home on the St Regis reservation in Hogansburg, NY. Dave got me involved with one of the local native box teams under the alias of Ralph Cree, who was not showing up for games. I was a person/player of some curiosity to neighbors and fans on the reservation and it became an inside joke to address me as "Ralph" during the remainder of my visit.

The following spring of 1973, I had worked my way into the mix for the first midfield on the varsity. It was the Wednesday before our first game that spring when the coaches (Cliff Stevenson and Bob Scalise, presently the AD at Harvard) told me to go back into the locker room and get a long pole. I switched to defense 72 hours before our opening game with the University of Virginia. My assignment that day was to cover some guy by the name of Tom Duquette. I came to discover afterwards that Tom was a senior at UVA and about to be selected as an All-American for the 4th time and a future Hall of Famer. It is better off that I did not know anything beforehand: he proceeded to show me some things I had not seen on the frozen parking lots of Rhode Island. It was a severe and comprehensive early education. Tom has since become a colleague and good friend.

• It was my second year as a head coach at Brown in 1984 when a young team made a trip to West Point to play Jack Emmer's Army team. It was also Dan Williams' first year at Army and the 6'5" rangy long stick middie played an intimidating center field in the Cadet's NINE LONG POLES ride. We were, obviously, struggling to clear the ball when my assistant, Michael O'Neil (Hopkins '78), turned to me and said "Coach, we need a time-out." My response was simply "don't you dare, I don't see anyone open either!" We lost 10-4.

• Brown played UMass in a re-scheduled game at the end of the 1990 regular season. It was Hall of Fame coach Dick Garber's 300th win and they buried us 21-18 behind Scott Hiller's eight goals. In an ironic twist, we were matched-up with UMass in a first round NCAA game in Amherst only a few days later. In an absolute deluge, we took a defenseman off the field and our two short stick defensive middies, Emio Zizza and Phil Maletta, took turns shutting off Scott. He was not happy and actually came over mid-game and complained directly, "Dom, this is not how the game is meant to be played!" Sorry Scott, held him to 0 & 0 and won the rematch 12-9. I can still picture Andy Towers sliding in the mud afterwards.

Our reward for this playoff win was a trip to the Dome two days later for a game with the #1 seed who had a bye in the first round. In addition, it was the final home game for Gary and Paul Gait. Our equipment was still wet when we unpacked for Friday's practice and our plan for the game was to slow down the pace in the first half and try to make a run at it in the second. A large excited crowd in attendance and Gary and Paul each had a goal in the game's first 14 seconds! So much for slowing it down, tweet, TIME-OUT…time to change the plan. Frankly, a valiant effort in a 20-12 loss.

• In 1993, my first spring in Charlottesville, I received a call from a UVA alumnus who informed me that ""I'm at a tournament in Baltimore, Coach, and you need to get up here and see this young player." This, in the years before the early recruiting, and I asked "how old is this kid?" When he told me "fifth grade," I told him I appreciated the call and would keep an eye out for the young man down the line. Johnny Christmas arrived for first year orientation at UVA almost nine years later.

Not long after, I received a call from a student at Gettysburg who asked about transferring to UVA for his third year. I did not see any way a D3 attackman could push Watson, Knight or Whiteley out of our line-up or that this 5'9"/170 athlete could survive as an ACC middie. I proceeded to tell him on multiple occasions that he was not likely to play for us and that he should reconsider his plans. He was so insistent and finally offered "you do not have to promise me anything, Coach, just give me a chance." I appreciated his determination and It did not take David Curry long to make an impression on our team. He may be the only player in NCAA history selected as a first team AA in both D1 and D3. David was also a US World Team player in '98. Sometimes we need to be careful not to outsmart ourselves!

• In the summer of 1995, the University of Virginia put natural grass down in Scott Stadium and built a small astroturf stadium adjacent to the football practice fields near to UHall. There had been some issues plowing Scott Stadium over the years and the Director of Field Services informed me that "we will not plow the new stadium." I told him that might be problematic for some early season games but we would have to make do with this new policy. That fall, in the week of the football game with Virginia Tech, there was a freak snow storm in Central Virginia. I happened to be flying back from a recruiting trip and as we passed over Charlottesville, I chuckled to see a shimmering, emerald field in a sea of white. It seems the football coach told the grounds crew, in no uncertain terms, to "get that field plowed right now." Amazing, really, from that day forward, the field became plowable!

• I have always said that if you are a lacrosse person and have trouble making friends, learn to string and fix sticks. There is no one who is quite as popular on a team. In turn, there are players who can only barely function unless their stick is perfect. Hall of Famer Doug Knight is neither of those folks. It was very near to the end of Friday's practice the day before our opening game with Syracuse in 1996. Doug walked over to me and held out his only stick whose plastic head had just broken. When he said to me "what do I do now?" the only suggestion that occurred to me was "here, try this" and I handed him mine. It made for a restless night considering that one of our leading players was about to play against the Orange with a stick he had barely thrown a pass with. Doug had eight goals the next day! He finished the season with 58 and was selected the National Player of the Year.

• It was 1997 and in the second half of that 22-21 classic game with Syracuse in the Dome. During a timeout, I leaned into the huddle and mentioned to everyone that "it was OK to slow this thing down." I am not sure how skillful I am at reading body language but any novice could have interpreted the unspoken signs that exclaimed in return "there is no frickin' way, Coach!"

• I had the entire team over to the house for a BBQ in the fall of 1998. I was sitting around with a couple of the older players later in the evening when Drew McKnight asked me if I "would shave off that mustache if we won the national championship?" I had grown the bushy mustache while playing box lacrosse in Montreal in 1975, which was only a couple of years since Virginia's previous championship (1972). I did not hesitate and informed those in attendance that "I would shave off anything they liked if we won the championship." It never occurred to me again until walking into the parking lot in College Park, having just beaten Syracuse to win that '99 Championship. Standing there were seniors Dave Bruce, David Baruch and Tucker Radebaugh holding a can of shaving cream and a pink Bic razor. My twins were bawling but I could not have been happier to be clean shaven for the first time in a quarter of a century!

We will save some others for another time.

Shaving off my moustache in the parking lot following
our first National Championship win in 1999

# 40

# Lighter Side of Lacrosse 2

Immediately upon graduation from Brown in 1974, I became the first assistant on the varsity for both soccer and lacrosse. You might think that a little surprising when you consider that I had never played nor seen lacrosse until arriving in Providence four years prior. What might be even more remarkable is that I don't recall that I had ever even kicked a soccer ball before that first day on the job. I worked hard to get up to speed with the soccer players, said "aqui" as often as possible when I wanted the ball and constantly looked for ways to make a meaningful contribution. We had a young, talented striker on the team by the name of Fred Pereira (who graduated as Brown's alltime leading scorer). In an early game that fall, a big back from Yale took Fred down hard near our bench. While everyone's attention was focused on Fred, I sidled up alongside the Yale player and informed him that "if you ever do that again, I will come back out here and drop you right where you stand." I was still working through some of my proper soccer protocols!

● Do you ever wonder why Canadian players who grow up playing box are such good finishers? Well, the goals are smaller and the goalies are padded properly and in the goal for almost every shot, in every shooting drill, in practice. Field players do not get to shoot live on goalies enough in their developmental years. I played in the original NLL in the summer of '75, drafted by legendary Canadian coach, Jim Bishop, on to the Montreal lesQuebecois. Our goalie was one of the best in that league, a Mohawk, Ernie Mitchell. When I used to come down the floor in practice, Ernie would start in with "C'mon Dom, c'mon," give me a little opening somewhere and then burst into laughter as he took it away every time. I'm glad he was enjoying himself; luckily, I had thick skin!

• Hall of Famer and '78 Hopkins grad, Mike O'Neil, was my first fulltime assistant at Brown, 1983-86. Michael was one of the great players and colorful characters in our game's history. He led Hopkins to a NCAA Championship in '78 against a Cornell team that had not lost a game in three years! During his three years in Providence, I do not think Mike ever paid to stay anywhere. His ability to talk people into taking care of him was absolutely uncanny. He spent his final spring in our house and I would tell you that his greatest skill would be making you feel comfortable with him in your home. I would walk in the door to find Michael waiting there to ask me, "Dom, how about some soup, can I get you some soup?" What a great guy, one of the people who touched me in the game. "Yes Michael, I'll have some soup!"

• It was a Monday during the early spring of '87 when I was informed by someone on the University side that a couple of our players had gotten into an altercation with some security guards at the weekend's hockey game. I stewed on this information until practice was winding down that afternoon. I told the players to get on the goal line extended, to run an 80 on every whistle and proceeded to "let them have it" with every sprint. It was pitch black by the time I ran out of expletives and was told later that they had run 48/80's.

• It was the following spring of 1988 when we played UPenn in a night game in Providence. Tony Seaman was upset before the game even began because he felt the lights were not adequate. I am sure Peter Smith, Penn's best attackman, thought the goalies couldn't see, he must have taken 30 shots! In a very dramatic affair, described by top D1 official Bob Schwalb as "one of the most intense games he had ever officiated," it was a low-scoring one-goal game with five minutes to play. Our attackman, Jamie Munro, came hard to the corner and bless his creative soul, I knew what he was likely to try. From my vantage point, it was "No, no Jamie, no, no...yes!" He stuck one behind his back in the far upper corner. We beat a semifinal Penn team 9-7.

• Jamie was our senior captain the next year and warming up for our game with Harvard with a BRAND-NEW stick. I had to pace over in the corner so as to not lose my mind and have a scene ten minutes before a critical game. Of course, Jamie had three goals in the game, played very well and we won our Ivy opener.

• The spring of 1993 was my first year at Virginia and we had a fair season, earned a trip to the NCAA playoffs. The regular season had just ended and our captain, Kevin Pehlke, was going to receive a prestigious award at the Athletic Department's season ending banquet. I did not want to ruin the surprise, simply told the team that everyone had to be at the dinner, unless they had an academic conflict. I was going to be out of town scouting potential playoff opponents. A half dozen of the players came to me to say that they had an exam study session as the same time as the banquet and asked if they could miss. I told them, "of course" and didn't think any more of it. The next day, I am sitting in my office and get a call from an old friend. Very innocently, he told me that he had seen six of our guys at a concert in Georgetown the night before. I told the six to come see me and when I asked how the study session had gone, to a man "really helpful coach, thanks a lot." I said, "good, because you are all suspended for the first round of the playoffs." When we got clobbered by an under manned club team two days later during our bye weekend and winning even a first-round playoff game seemed unlikely, I was certain I was about to be fired in my first year. Four of the six who sat out were regulars and the remaining players rose up to win that NCAA game 25-9.

● It was the spring of 1994 when we established a two-mile run time as the standard to begin practice that spring. Each player ran his two-miles on the track in the fall and we negotiated an individual time for each player to meet upon his return in January. It certainly seemed a fairer method than having the same standard for everyone on the team. I am happy to report that only one player did not make his time, a big, strong football player who was close, but couldn't get there. The rule was you could not practice until you made the time and everyone felt bad for Chris Morton, who ran it every day for almost a week. We were all frustrated and then, I had an idea. We had not specified that you had to run it on a track and we measured off a two mile route that began at the top of Observatory Hill, a steep half-mile long incline on campus. We took Chris to the top and pushed him off this new runway…he made his time!

• It was the Wednesday before our 1995 semifinal game with Syracuse. My wife had been bugging me for some time to have the team doctor look at a small lump on the side of my face, just below my ear. It finally occurred to me and the doctor called over to the Dermatology Dept. at the University Hospital. It was only an hour or two before practice but when the chairman of the Department of Dermatology agreed to see me, I hustled over. He diagnosed a basal cell and offered to cut it out on the spot. I told him I was in a hurry but a couple of shots to numb the area, snip, tug, eight stitches, a band aid and flying out the door. I ran right out to the practice field and starting my normal barking at the players during our pre-practice drills. When I saw enough guys standing around, staring, with their mouths agape, I finally asked, "what the hell is going on?" One of the older guys pointed at me and I realized I had popped the stitches and had blood running down my neck into my shirt! I couldn't feel it with the novacain still in play. They fixed me back up but we still couldn't cover Roy Colsey!

• We brought an excellent starting attack, Jay Jalbert, Drew McKnight and Tucker Radebaugh. back to the team in the fall of 1998. Conor Gill was also on his way to campus for his freshman year and we needed to move someone to the midfield. Probably too big an adjustment for a freshman, we needed Tuck's left hand on the field all the time and Drew was to miss fall lacrosse with shoulder surgery. Jay was none too happy to hear that he was the one and was dragged a little kicking and screaming to the face-off wing. He went on to be a first team All-American that spring, the USILA Midfielder of the Year and we captured Virginia's first National Championship in 27 years! We both smile about it now.

Jay Jalbert, April 2000

• In the spring of 2005, we played Hopkins in one of the most exciting NCAA semifinal games in tournament history. We found ourselves down 6-1, tied it, went ahead, sat through one of the most dramatic 50 minute rain-delays, Kyle Harrison immediately tied it, we went ahead again with 12 seconds to play only to have Hopkins tie it and send us into overtime. We had three great shots on our first possession but Hopkins came down the field with their defensive middies still on the field. With every fiber of my being, I am convinced that we might still be playing if Dave (Pietramala) hadn't used his timeout earlier in the overtime. As it was, SSDM Benson Erwin took the shot and scored his fourth goal of the season to send his team to the national championship game!

• With time-outs in mind…it was the spring of 2009 and a game between Virginia and Maryland at Klockner Stadium. We had played a lot of close games with the Terps over the years and a casual fan might have predicted this one tied and going into overtime. These games are generally settled quickly and it was a bit of a surprise as this one went to a second OT, a 3rd, 4th, 5th, 6th and 7th. Coach Cottle and I used every available time-out allowed throughout the first six overtimes. At one point, I seem to recall telling the team, "remember what we told you the last time…well, do it better this time!" Maryland had the ball first in the seventh OT, our goalie Adam Ghitelman gathered possession and as we went down the field, I turned to Coach VanArsdale and said, "don't call it, let's see what happens." Brian Carroll split to his left hand off the top and sunk the winner. Sometimes, we are just better off getting out of the way.

• It was the summer of 2011 and I was invited to the ESPY Award Show in California as a candidate for Coach of the Year.

I would admit to never being a "clothes horse" and would generally describe my style as "casually uninformed." The parents got together and identified the one (Gary Gill) who had the nerve to ask me to please buy a decent suit. In a case of a reverse NCAA recruiting violation, the parents sent me a gift certificate to make it happen!

I hope you enjoyed reading these as much as I enjoyed recalling them!

# 41

## Lovingly Chaotic

As I walked in the front door to the Edell household this past Saturday, I could hear Dick in a back room talking on the phone. As it turns out, he was catching up with his former assistant and present UAlbany head coach, Scott Marr. It is not unusual for coaching friends of Dick's to reach out only hours before their opening faceoff (in this case on the road against Vermont).

There were people everywhere. Two of Dick's children, a daughter-in-law and grandchildren were scattered throughout. An hour in, another daughter, Krissy, contributed a couple more grandchildren and a black lab to the mayhem. With me and good Edell family friend (and old Brown teammate) Jeff Wagner added in, it took a mother's strength for Dolores to maintain some order. When I was offered a coke that turned out to be as flat as could be imagined, I accused Dick of pilfering it from the 1991 tailgate following Maryland's win in the NCAA quarterfinals against my undefeated Brown team. And, if Steve Kavovit is out there listening, you should know that Dick attributes your 29 saves in that game mostly to the fact that we "just hit him"!

I have been to Dick's a number of times during these past few years. My life has been graced to have been in the presence of Bob Scott, Jim Adams, Bill Tanton, Ira Hochstadt, Dave Urick, Tony

Seaman, Buddy Beardmore, Bill Sbarra, Marc VanArsdale and others during these visits. It has been my very humble pleasure to sit and simply listen to these gentlemen talk about their lives in the game. You cannot help but be impressed by the unflinching eagerness to come spend the time with Dick. I often talk with young players about the sense of community that still exists within our game. It is not to be taken for granted and is still an enduring characteristic even as lacrosse has expanded beyond its provincial borders.

With all due respect, this was not a day for tales of hallowed Homewood homilies. This was the day before Dick's 73rd birthday and you were best served bringing an irreverent spirit and a thick skin to this opening act. Thoughts of that '91 playoff game were triggered when the most recent Brown/Harvard game came on the screen. Dick seemed to recall in sharp detail that the Brown fans knew some things about his family background that he was not aware of! He also described turning to assistant Dave Slaskofsky during the game and having a Brown fan's head thrust between them. I told him on more than one occasion that I found it unlikely that my Ivy League brothers would act in such a coarse manner. Dick remembers everything and could rattle off things about my teams and players that I had long forgotten. We had a good laugh, turned to Navy/Loyola on the screen and had four hours just fly by.

Even before the events that occurred in my life this past spring, my visits with Dick may have been more therapeutic for me than they were for him. It is only his body that is wheelchair bound. His spirit is consumed with family and friends, lacrosse memories and a generosity that draws us all in. He is "Big Man" and I have been blessed that my life's journey has brought me close to his magical touch. His diminishing physical strength is not an insignificant part of this story but it only barely touches the lasting tale of this good man.

As I am walking out the door, in the chaos of Dick yapping at the dog to get away from the table, with grandchildren banging into his chair and the Army/Holy Cross telecast in the background, I look over to see Dick mouth the words "I love you"... thank you Big Man.

# 42

## Another Perspective

Somehow, we seem to have survived the apocalyptic coming and going of September 1st. Almost hard to imagine we are still going to have college sports and a lacrosse season and that colleges themselves are still standing after the seismic eruptions predicted by the change in the recruiting legislation. Let me go so far as to offer this suggestion...if the initial date for recruiting contact was December 1st of their "senior" year, most of the best prospects would still be going to UNC, Duke, Virginia and Notre Dame, the majority of the "next level" players with solid grades would be looking at the Patriot League and the best upstate New York prospects would still think that the Dome was the center of the lacrosse universe. I have always considered that most players would find their way to the same schools if the recruiting was even more severely limited. The subtle but not insignificant shift that accompanies this current change is the that the recruiting will not continue to get earlier and high school students should enjoy an uninterrupted freshmen year.

I have also been hearing that these new rules will accelerate a scenario where prospects need to attend lacrosse events in the fall in lieu of participation in football and soccer. Let me suggest to high school players and their parents that every reputable college coach that I know would prefer you play a fall sport. There is nothing you can do for your development as a lacrosse player on your own that is better than going to football and soccer practice every day. You learn and strengthen the fundamental understanding of lacrosse team offense and defense on the football and soccer fields, the basketball courts and hockey rinks of your youth. The spring and summer following your sophomore year of high school will give the college coaches ample time and opportunity to make a thorough evaluation of your potential. Do you have a school or two that stands head and shoulders above the rest in your plans? Give up one of your club tournaments and go to camp or a prospect day at that institution. That is still the best setting for college coaches to appreciate the subtle nuances of your game.

To the college coaches, I am going to make this thorny recommendation—do not contact players who are committed to other schools. These commitments will come a little later now, let's consider them at least slightly more mature decisions than before the new legislation. This talk about an increased frequency of "poaching" seems to carry an air of inevitability. It does not have to be that way. Men's and women's lacrosse has already taken a leadership role on the college landscape with an uncommon cooperation and creative spirit that distinguishes the new rules. The college coaches could also decide that they simply will not make an initial contact with a committed athlete. Could a young man change his mind in his junior or senior year?…yes, of course, but don't initiate that contact and let common decency and an "honor among thieves" carry the day.

Why bother stepping up to this complicated issue? I have always felt strongly that it does matter that the college coaches respect and trust each other. You could make an argument that

Alabama football or (to a lesser extent) Duke basketball affects every aspect of life at those respective institutions. Virginia Lacrosse does not. The primary consideration for a college lacrosse program is to provide a life-changing/sustaining experience for the participants. Did they grow up in their four years? Did they become better citizens? Will they be better husbands and fathers because of their relationship to you and the experience of playing college lacrosse? If there is any truth here, college coaches need to use every opportunity to strengthen the core values that will characterize this development. The relationship that begins with the encouragement to break your word and the premise that disloyalty has no consequence is without foundation and will likely have a contagious effect throughout your program.

If you stood up at the next coaches meeting and humbly declared that "I'm not going down this road," I believe you would feel better about yourself, build respect among your peers, be an inspiration to your players and, in the end, be even more of a winner.

Thanks.

# 43

## "Where's My Ring?"

Having been fortunate to be part of some Championship teams, there is always a little bit of a question afterwards about who will receive a championship ring. I am sure that most coaches who find themselves faced with that fortuitous dilemma lean toward my general feeling, which was "give one to everyone who helped us along the way." I would be including managers, trainers, equipment and sports information staff, the grounds crew, and would have kept going had my sports administrator not said "enough." While a recognition of thankfulness, someone was still paying the bill for all these celebratory trimmings.

In retrospect, one group I never considered in this category was the former head coaches at my institution, especially those who never had won a championship, for any number of reasons, during their tenure. They were certainly an influence on the evolution of the program at our institution and likely a significant professional influence on my own career. If I ever find myself in that situation again, it will certainly bear some consideration.... which leads me to Andy Shay.

I am not sure that Andy knows this, I am not sure that there is any reason for Andy to know this, and there are few people besides my wife who recall that I was the head coach at Yale....

for a day. It was the summer of 1980 and Bob McHenry had just retired after ten years as the head Bulldog. I had been the first assistant at Brown for six years and was excited to submit my name as a candidate. The Yale AD at the time was Frank Ryan, an unlikely combination of former QB for the Cleveland Browns and a math PhD. During the interview process, it was explained to me that the position would be combined with being the defensive backfield coach for varsity football. I was slightly in awe to meet in a darkened office with the iconic Yale head football coach, Carm Cozza. I explained to Coach Cozza that I had not been around football for almost ten years, since last playing as a junior at Brown. He said it was no problem, that they would teach me what I needed to know and that they would welcome me to the staff. I walked away impressed but also a little perplexed feeling that this was almost as much about football as lacrosse. I was offered the position soon thereafter and a young coach, about to start a family, in need of a raise and new professional challenges, accepted the offer.

I was working a camp in New England at the time and went directly from New Haven back to the camp, now as the new head coach at Yale. My head was slightly spinning from the day's activities and from the congratulations of all the other staff people on my new position. In a quiet moment later that evening, Dick Garber came by to see me. Dick was the head coach at UMass, won 300 games in his career (beat my Brown team for #300) and is now in the National Hall of Fame. More importantly, he was one of the most respected coaches in our profession and I considered him a mentor and role model, on and off the field. While he watched everyone congratulating me throughout the day, in that quiet moment he asked, "what's wrong?" He caught me by surprise and I replied "what do you mean?" He said, "Dom, you don't seem that happy." I hesitated but told him that I really did not want to be a football coach and felt that may have been Yale's priority. He said "don't take it, Dom, you're good and something better suited will come along." I had never really considered that option and went to bed more confused than excited.

I woke early the next morning, called Mr. Ryan and told him that I needed to come see him. We sat out back at his house and I tried to explain that I was flattered to be considered as a coach in Yale's powerhouse football program but that I really wanted to be a lacrosse coach. I offered to coach the freshmen football team for a couple of years until we got the lacrosse program up and running and then switch over to the varsity. He suggested we do the opposite, start on the varsity football and if things really don't work out with lacrosse, we'll switch you over to the frosh level. With Dick's quiet voice in my head, I had made up my mind and politely declined the offer. Mike Waldvogel accepted the position shortly thereafter and did a great job.

The very next summer of 1981, I was the finalist for the Princeton job but did not get offered. Following that disappointment, I walked in to the Brown AD's office and informed John Parry that I was going to get out of coaching. I wasn't angry but I had not gotten the job I wanted and felt that my career as an assistant had run its course. He proceeded to tell me he had an idea, asked that I wait a month and then announced that I would be the next head coach at Brown beginning in the fall of 1982. Thus began my ten years as the head coach at Brown and the preparation that went into our moving to Charlottesville in the summer of 1992.

I tell young people all the time that my simply standing in front of them is the clearest example of "Anything's Possible" and "You Never Know." Work hard, be honest, treat the people around you as if they are family…things will work out, probably just as they are supposed to.

In the meantime, that's about a size 10, Andy!

# 44

## Not In The Hall Of Fame

I was speaking with my brother in law, David Lasagna, recently about the selection by our Hall of Fame Committee of the Navy '65 team as our "Team of Distinction," to be honored by US Lacrosse on this coming September 28th. His father, Dr. Louis Lasagna, was a brilliant young doctor at Johns Hopkins and David (Peter's older brother) had nearly grown up on Homewood Field. He would interrupt any discussion of Navy's dominance with some variation of "man, you should have seen Joe Cowan." Having never seen Cowan but having heard tales, I believed him. To strengthen his Hopkins' argument I offered, "and I guess that Charlie Coker was pretty good too." David's response of "Who?" caught me completely off guard. Is it possible to have been so pre-occupied with Cowan that someone would fail to even recognize a 2x 1st team AA middie who played alongside him for two years? The answer is, obviously, yes and I began to think of other players in my lifetime who fall into a similar situation.

We have National Hall of Famers and enjoy imagining our "Greatest of All Time" selections. For purposes of this moment in history, I am proposing a new category of recognition…"All-time team of players/characters not presently in the Hall of Fame, generally overlooked in that process but, who had the talent to be considered, may have had their career cut short by injury or circumstance, may have toiled in the land of lacrosse obscurity or played in the shadow of more famous teammates…lacrosse fans don't recall or know enough about, guys who couldn't be covered, held teams together or who would take your lunch money as you got off the bus." I have to have seen them play (last 48 years), except for Coker, and no short stick defensive middies allowed, since the whole team could be about the Jeff Reynolds, Jack Near's, Chris Schiller, JJ Morrissey's and Billy Glading's of the world. Since I always consult with Marc VanArsdale (4 NC's at Hobart, 2x Finals MVP) on questions of lacrosse history, you may detect a little upstate New York bias. The fact that the discussion began with consideration of a 2x 1st team AA from Hopkins overlooked by a Baltimore lacrosse fan may have to serve as balancing the field.

I continue to be amazed that Jason Coffman, Salisbury, '96 and Carthage, NY, is not in the Hall of Fame…all-time NCAA scorer, 4x 1st team AA, 2 NC's and scored ten goals in his first college game against Roanoke…one word to describe, tough. How about Tim Whiteley, Virginia '96? Tim played between Hall of Famers Mike Watson and Doug Knight, played primarily in his off-hand and was a coach on the field. You might pick him first if you were putting a team together. Randy Lunblad, Syracuse '84, a lot like Tim, a key player on their first National Championship team, suffered a bad knee injury after that first season and was never quite able to follow-up. Peter Worstell, Maryland '81 was a 4x AA for the Terps at two different positions. I thought Peter may have been the most electrifying player at the US Team tryouts in 1977. However, he did not make that team and a knee injury interfered with the second half of his college career. Finally, how many of you can tell me about Mike Perkins? Mike was a wildly athletic attackman who graduated as Cortland's alltime leading scorer in 1985, selected MVP as a frosh, 4 years with 50 points and a 2x 1st team AA. How about post D3? Mike was the leading scorer for the Syracuse Spirit of the American Lacrosse League before it folded.

In the middle of the field, we started with Coker, who also played football and wrestled at Hopkins. Next to the established pedigree of Coker stands one of the most dynamic players of my lifetime, John Fay, New Hampshire '81. John mysteriously appeared out of the woods of Maine (actually Concord Carlisle, MA) and fans cannot quite fathom that his one-hand shot on the run, with either hand, was a legitimate scoring opportunity. I am not sure of a stronger, more physical dodger in the game. Tim Soudan, UMass '90 and Craig Jaeger, Cornell '78 were close and an earlier Big Red alum, Bob Shaw, was simply one of the most solid, best all-around middies for Cornell's first National Championship team in 1971. How about Doug Shanahan, Hofstra '01, the very first Tewaaraton recipient and an NFL candidate? Consider trying to cover a midfield of Fay, Shanahan and Jaeger as they rolled out of the box! One of the best groundball, two-way middies was Jimmy Buczek, '92, who was a key member of North Carolina's powerhouse early 90's teams. More recently, it is very hard to imagine that Zach Currier, Princeton '17 was not a 1st team AA selection. He was other-worldly off the ground. I thoroughly enjoyed watching the flowing blond locks of Hobart's Beaver Draffen, '75 and the facing off and all-around play of Adelphi's Gordon Purdie '89. The Adelphi middie I could really just stand off to the side and watch had the perfect name, Kirk Jurgelevich, '75. I was happy to stand off to the side because you did not want to slide to Kirk, a knot of muscle who went directly to the goal.

The first defenseman who comes to mind is Mark Farnham, Brown '80. Mark had never seen lacrosse before his freshman year and played about a month on the JV. He saw limited time as a soph on the varsity. The next year he was selected 2$^{nd}$ team AA and the Ivy League Player of the Year. He went on to be the only defenseman ever selected as MVP of the North-South game and may still have the quickest hands and feet I have ever seen on a lacrosse field. There are always players who really blossom after college and Steve Holmes of Virginia falls into that category. Steve's burning desire to play for the Philadelphia Eagles interfered with his college career but ask MLL players if there was a better athlete in the league these past ten years. Gary Clipp, '77 was a 2x 1$^{st}$ team AA selection at UMBC but it is even more notable that he was selected 9x All-Club for Mt Washington and MLC before the MLL was in play. John Pirro, Roanoke '77 passed in 2013 but left a legacy as a 3x 1$^{st}$ team AA and 2x National Defenseman of the Year. Back to Hobart for a second… Tim Clark '87 was the NCAA representative for men's lacrosse for many years. As an undergraduate, he was an absolute shut-down bulldog of a defender as a freshman and into his soph year when a horrific knee injury sidelined him until returning as a captain in his senior year.

It is hard to hide top goalie play since their performance so often distinguishes final results, Rick Blick '78 and Guy VanArsdale '84 of Hobart may both wind up in the Hall of Fame one day. Quint Kessenich, Rodney Rullman and Greg Cattrano may be considered more for the body of their work in the game rather than just a college career. In a more recent era of John

Mark Farnham receiving N-S MVP from Richie Moran, 1980

Galloway, Adam Ghitelman and Tyler Fiorito, I might choose TC DiBartolo, Mount St Mary's '11 as the best stopper of the group.

You might think this the ending to our inaugural process of selecting our "overlooked heroes" but if it was fitting to start with Charlie Coker, it may be even more fitting to end with, perhaps, the finest player at his position who ever streaked across the lacrosse universe. With all due respect to Mike Farrell, who may have invented the position, Steve Mitchell, who defined it, Kyle Sweeney, who refined it and Michael Ehrhardt, who may be the next generation, the best long stick middie I have ever seen is Steve Kisslinger of Adelphi/Towson. I have never seen a defenseman take the ball off good middies more consistently and turn defensive situations into offensive opportunities more quickly. He was simply a terror in the middle of the field.

Fire away…I am sure I missed a number of others. We will be looking for candidates for our second class!

> Second Class:
> Tom Carmean – A — AUMass
> Mark Douglas – A — Maryland
> Jim Trenz – A — Penn State/Cornell
> Andy Towers – M — Brown
> Doug Shanahan – M — Hofstra
> Mike Page - M — Penn
> FO – Alex Smith — Delaware
> Ric Beardsley – D — Syracuse
> Brett Hughes – D — Virginia

# 45

## Is That What We Are Doing?!

Yeah, yeah, yeah, I have heard and agree with most of the arguments that criticize the "participation trophy" mentality surrounding today's youth. However, when you are north of 65 years of age, any recognition hardware that involves physical exertion will land in an esteemed place on my mantle piece.

Let me back-up. I graduated from Brown in 1974, played almost ten years of club lacrosse with Brine (Bob Shillinglaw, Tom Cafaro, Jeff Wagner...) until just about the time that I became a head coach at Brown and my middle child was born in the early 80s. It seemed like we played the Long Island Lacrosse Club (Alan Lowe, Tom Postel, Stan Kowalski, Ron Fraser...) in the northern Finals almost every year and I recall that the post-game fellowship was a valued element of the exercise.

I hadn't played any lacrosse for most of the next ten years when I received a call from my former Brown roommate and Mohawk Indian, David White. He asked if I would be interested in playing on a team of upstate NY Native Americans and high school coaches in the master's division of a tournament in Lake Placid that had begun play the year before. I was now close to 40 years of age but we were already in the Adirondacks at an annual

Playing for the Brine Lacrosse Club, 1979

family gathering. Thought I would give it a try and joined a team called the "North Country Legends."

The first game I played in, I recall so vividly thinking to myself, "Hey, I still got it." Then, sitting on the sideline watching a game with other teams in our division, I was flabbergasted with the impression "Is that what we are doing?...oh, my god, that's pathetic." But, it turned out to be a lot of fun, a good bunch of guys, we won the division that first year and I was hooked. I played for most of the next 16-17 years until deciding that I didn't need to get hurt approaching my 60th birthday. I retired from playing and it was almost as if it was traded for a week at the beach in Ocean City, MD. Well, I got hurt in the surf at the beach that first year away, had my shoulder operated on and figured, "what the heck, if I'm going to get hurt at the beach, I might as well just keep playing lacrosse!" So, I have played these past few years in the Ultra Grand Master's (older than dirt!)

Playing in Lake Placid, 2009

Division of 60 years of age and older. Someone asked me what the play is like in this division and I described it thus...there is a groundball off to the side, just a few feet away, let's take a moment to consider our options and the possible consequences here before making a commitment.

I think most of us walk away (when we get to walk away!) from each year's tournament thinking that we are going to get in better shape and be more of a force the next year. Of course, that's impossible as we get older and each year's difference in age with the younger guys in our division is actually measured in dog years! I always thought of Brooks Sweet (going into the National Hall of Fame in Sept) as a young boy and he scored the winner against us in his first year in this oldest division in a January tournament in Florida.

This most recent Lake Placid Tournament was winding down in an eerily similar fashion to years past. Our Legends team got

With Brown classmate, roommate, teammate and close
friend Dave White in Lake Placid, 2009

through the round robin play undefeated and was set to play the Cloudsplitters in the Championship game. Truth be told, the "Splitters" have dominated the division in recent years and beat us in exactly the same scenario in '16. Just before the face-off, in what would have been the last game of the day, the skies opened and the fields were flooded and unplayable. Talk of re-scheduling was drowned out by a (Legends) proposal to simply declare co-champions. Let's see now…no one gets hurt, both teams share a beer in the parking lot instead and everyone goes home a winner…no contest, co-champions it is. And, if you drop the "co" in your recollections with friends, who is the wiser? Finally, to my Splitter comrades…we would not have beaten you that badly.

# 46

# The History of Automatic Qualifiers

I served on the Men's Lacrosse Executive Committee from 1997 till 2001. Terms are generally for four years and I do not recall why I was asked to stay on for a fifth. My first correspondence as a member of the committee was with a fan who accused me of "the old boys club" mentality for leaving an undefeated Bucknell team out of the 2006 Tournament field. Since I was not a member of the committee during that selection process, I considered myself rudely inducted into an environment that intersected unwittingly with the passion of college fans.

During my time on the committee, we were charged with both the selection of teams and organization of the NCAA Tournament and consideration of rule changes. I have often said that those five years were my official growing up period as a college lacrosse coach. There were serious decisions that needed to be made that involved the rules of play and excluding friends and peers from post-season play. The committee worked very hard to be fair but, no matter, there was always going to be someone left out. In addition and, in a timely, ironic twist, it was our committee that voted the dive out of the game (for many of the reasons we are struggling with its adjudication presently), voted in a shot clock and approved the concept of automatic qualification to the NCAA Tournament for conference champions. The college coaches pressured the committee to reconsider the implementation of the clock more than 15 years ago and the introduction of automatic qualifiers was not without its own controversy.

This is truly "Tournament Week" in college lacrosse…4-6 teams in every conference involved in post-season play, the Patriot League going to an expanded model in 2020, the Ivy League in The Big Apple, the ACC giving their final game participants a week to prepare, etc., almost half the teams in Division 1 still have a shot at their conference title. With all this in mind, it may be hard to imagine that it was a complicated decision in 2000 to consider the AQ model. Each conference was represented on the committee and I was the Atlantic Coast Conference representative. In those days, the four ACC teams, Hopkins and Syracuse were almost "an automatic" to make the NCAA Tournament. In a stagnant twelve team field, however, the addition of automatic qualifiers was going to significantly reduce the number of at-large opportunities. While our committee approved a proposal to the NCAA to increase the size of the field from 12 to 16 teams at the same time, there was no guarantee of its passage. I saw the implementation of AQs as good for the game, giving more teams access to the NCAA Tournament. I think we have seen overall in these past nineteen years what we hoped would happen. Institutions in more remote areas have added lacrosse and many of them have increased their support for their programs overall. At the same time, the traditional powers that had carried and grown the game in its history were in danger of losing some access. As the representative of these schools, my vote was a pivotal one within the committee, interpreted as an approval to push the proposal forward. However, the acclaim for my magnanimity was not universal. The range of responses from the traditional powers extended from concern to a harsh rebuke from the Maryland AD. She implied in a letter that the NCAA would never approve tournament expansion and it would hurt the ACC.

I was still mostly just a lacrosse coach and it was unsettling to be roundly criticized by my peers for a decision intended to help the game. You can imagine my relief when the NCAA moved unexpectedly to approve an increase in the tournament field from 12 to 16 in 2002. In retrospect, the game did benefit from the adoption of automatic qualification and seems more exciting than ever. It was a process that rewarded a little leap of faith.

# 47

# 2017 Convention Thoughts

I am sitting here at my desk, watching the first snowfall of the season, having just returned last evening from the 2017 USILA/IMLCA meetings. Two things came together for me on the extended rush hour drive home. I was humbled and honored to have received the Frenchy Julien Award for Service at the Nike luncheon and chuckled every time I ran into an old friend who did a recognition double-take with my new bearded look. The last time this happened was in 1999 after that team shaved off a bushy mustache I had been sporting for the previous 25 years.

Here is how a service award and facial hair became related to a consideration of our coaching lives. If I was giving my acceptance remarks today, I would begin with, "To all the young coaches in attendance." The narrative would go on to recall how I always came away from these meetings so excited about the start of the season. I can easily remember being so consumed by the pursuit of winning, the championships, the gold ring and…there is nothing wrong with that. You can pursue success while still being primarily concerned with the quality of your influence. You need to remain vigilant but, it can be done. Fair or not, however, winning enriches the relationships among the participants while remaining a professional requirement. To have a fulfilling career in college coaching, you need to find a formula for success.

Let me also tell you that winning the national championship is not as unceasingly satisfying as people might imagine. It is a relief, first and foremost, for the coaches and programs for which it is an expectation. The very next day after we won our first championship in '99, Virginia's first in 27 years, I drove 8 hours to get to the state sectional high school playoffs at Coyne Field in Syracuse. It was walking into that stadium where I ran into acquaintances who did not initially recognize me without the mustache. It felt good to know we had won the day before but it occurred to me that we were slightly behind in the recruiting and I was struck by the irony of it all.

I coached at the college level for 42 years and have had these past 18 months to consider closely that time spent. I am here to confirm for you that the existential joy in our lives comes from helping others. That may happen for you through your experience at work. When a player on Jon Torpey's High Point team asked me to quantify the successes in my career, I told him frankly that Zed Williams' graduation from Virginia sits beside anything we accomplished on the field. We all have those stories in our lives and our true mission is to create a setting where we can be inspired by these young men every day.

I am also suggesting to you that you have more time than you think. The old adage "if you want something done, give it to a busy man" applies to college coaches as well as to any group. Look for opportunities to reach out. I mean more than simply fulfilling your institutional community service obligation. Being a college coach gives you a platform, people will listen, you can help people, you can affect change in their lives. When I asked Charley

Toomey and Ryan Polley to serve on regional advisory boards for Harlem Lacrosse, I understood their hesitation. Would it get in the way of what they were trying to accomplish at Loyola and BU? They have already contributed so much more to the organization than they likely imagined and I would hope that their lives are richer for the effort. They have made a meaningful difference in their urban communities.

I am old enough to have known Frenchy Julien, proud to receive this service award in his name and encourage all of you, during this holiday season, to look for opportunities to serve the greater good. You will win even more in your life than the scoreboard proclaims.

# 48

# I'm Not Interested in "Grow the Game"

I have gotten around to speak with a lot of young lacrosse players in recent days. I am always emphasizing to them that the road to their development in the game includes mastering the fundamentals, listening to your coaches, learning to be a great passer, playing other sports and, most importantly, aspiring to be a leader among your peers. In order to truly reach this final goal, a young player would need to develop and exhibit all the leadership qualities we have talked about previously...fearlessness, selflessness, honesty, work ethic and self-discipline. A young player willing to embody these aspirational goals could not help but also become an athlete approaching his true competitive, playing potential. You are not sacrificing individual development, you are enhancing it.

When I was first introduced to Harlem Lacrosse 5-6 years ago, it was the founder, Simon Cataldo, who said to me that the primary mission of the organization was to "grow the child." HL was developing a model that used lacrosse to reach underserved young men and women in the inner city. While I was mystified to consider that our sport was such an effective tool in this unlikely environment, I quickly came to appreciate that a young person with some proper mentoring and coaching learns to love this game like any kid growing up in Baltimore or Long Island. Harlem Lacrosse's determination of their own success was not calculated by counting heads. It was actually by whether or not they were changing lives and…one at a time was fine.

So, an individual athlete who aspires to lead enhances his individual development without obsessing about it and Harlem Lacrosse is growing the game amongst a population that never would have found it without considering the sport's overall growth as only a secondary goal of the organization. This premise of unintended consequences has struck a chord. While our game continues to be one of the only sports still growing nationally, its growth rate has slowed. Is this a permanent adjustment or a temporary hiatus? US Lacrosse has moved into new headquarters and is always searching for methods to increase exposure, club coaches and a new entrepreneurial class in lacrosse look to combine an increased growth in numbers with a flourishing bottom line, the MLL, the NLL and the UWLX are looking for new fans to drive attendance, TV coverage, lacrosse networks and a social media blitz have not produced the anticipated, consistently dramatic increases in participation.

It is understandable that industry leaders anguish over this incremental growth. The answer to questions of investment in research and development, sponsorships, facilities, etc. arrives as an educated guess about the state of the game in the future. What if the development of sustainable growth in the game needs an evolving model, with innovative priorities? As I search for those activities, in this post-coaching life, where I can still have influence in the game, I find myself drawn again to Simon's early call…"grow the child." Although my recent travels throughout the lacrosse world have brought me into contact with a strikingly diverse range of teams, coaches, fans and administrators, I corrected a recent host who introduced me as "having done so much for the growth of the game." I was struck at that very moment with an overwhelming sense that this was not my priority. I wasn't there to spread the gospel or to simply give a motivational talk. I wanted to actually help a coach, reach a young person, I wanted to change someone's life, make the world a slightly better place. Giving speeches, handing out sticks, stickers, copies of a magazine, etc. can be a benevolent (and necessary) introduction to the game. I wanted more, however, by focusing on less. While it is not wrong to gauge success on increased profits and registration numbers, the appeal of our game has always embraced a more personal connection. You do not have to blow up the corporate model and, indeed, need everyone's best effort. But, let's be mindful of the game's higher calling. Seize on the spirituality of lacrosse by trying to change a life. Extend yourself to someone in need, follow-up with a young person after practice, offer to become a mentor, a big brother/sister, be a tutor, write a letter of support, call that person back, meet someone for lunch, etc. How about retired coaches offering their expertise to urban program directors and students once a week, once a month? In addition to the Harlem Lacrosse programs in NYC, Philly, Boston, Balt and LA, there is OWLS Lacrosse in Chicago, Rosemary Hills in DC, City Lax in both New York and Denver and USL urban start-ups in Albany and Cleveland. Could USL act as the broker who puts college programs/coaches and former players together with these urban institutions? Wagner College could "adopt" one of these NYC schools, Hofstra another, Boston College and BU in Beantown, UPenn and Drexel, UMBC and Loyola, Richmond, Northwestern, etc. Imagine a college freshman being assigned an urban high school freshman in pursuit of an individual relationship. How about all the NYC lacrosse/finance guys getting themselves organized to help coach, mentor and/or monitor a study hall once a month? We might really make a difference in someone's life, the potential seems limitless. I realize that I am not as busy as I used to be, but there is a wise saying, "if you want something done, give it to a busy man." This may just be a reminder for those of us who grew up in the game. There is a greater chance to develop a sustainable, positive model for lacrosse if we inspire each other to grow the game one act of kindness at a time.

# 49

## Season of Giving

Whenever I am presented with an opportunity to speak with younger lacrosse players, I always talk about the sense of community within our game. It is a very real phenomenon not readily found within the foundation of many other similarly diverse organizations. I truly believe it has to do with the Native American roots of the game and the spirituality that accompanies our participation. There is a "Spirit in the Stick" (author Neil Duffy) that extends throughout a life in the game. I am forever repeating the mantra that "if you treat the game with respect, it can be your friend for a long time."

I have two true stories that touched my life through a relationship with the game that seem appropriately shared during this late November Season of Giving. If you believe in some form of spiritual accounting, you might consider them related to each other and to a more profound authority than I can adequately articulate.

The first happened around the spring of 1990. It was after 11:00 pm and my wife Krissy and I were already in bed. The phone unexpectedly rang and the caller said "Coach, you don't know who I am but I know your name through lacrosse and there was no one else for me to call. I really need a favor. My teenage daughter has just flown in to the Providence Airport and her connecting flight to Martha's Vineyard has been cancelled. She is too young to check into a hotel. Could you please check her into a hotel and then she can take care of the rest?" I told him I would take care of it, dressed, drove the twenty minutes out to the airport, picked her up, brought her back to the house, put her in the guest room, brought her back to the airport in the morning and never thought more of it. When a gift basket arrived a few days later, I thought it a nice gesture, end of story.

It turns out that we were looking to move to Charlottesville, Virginia, less than two years later. The young woman we picked up at the airport was Paige Perriello and the voice on the phone was her father Dr. Vito Perriello. The Perriellos lived in Charlottesville and Vito was a pediatrician with a specific interest in children with cognitive disabilities, of which I had two at the time, six year old identical twin girls, Maggie and Emma. Vito became our pediatrician until our four children outgrew his service and his untimely passing from a massive stroke in 2013. If that is not enough, Paige, who played lacrosse and graduated from Princeton in 1994, took over her father's practice and was the pediatrician for my two grandsons, Lil' Dom and Luigi. The Perriellos remain good friends.

The second story began in the summer of 1992. I had just accepted the head coaching position at the University of Virginia and was in the middle of working the final session of our lacrosse camp at Brown. I was on the field when my phone rang. It was my father, who had just been admitted to North Shore Hospital on Long Island. I knew he was going in for a stress test that day but the doctor had implied that it was just a formality. He had been experiencing some pain in his left shoulder but he was a big man, a former New York City cop and a self-employed general contractor. The doctor thought my father's discomfort was likely arthritis but scheduled the stress test for six weeks later as a precaution. They stopped the test halfway through and told my dad that he needed bypass surgery and that he needed it the very next day. My father was calling me from the hospital and very anxiously asking what he should do. Should he trust this doctor that he barely knew or take a chance, walk away and gather some additional opinions? Midway through our conversation he interrupted to say, "wait a minute, Dom, another doctor just entered the room and I will call you back." When he called back half an hour later, he had some surprising news. This new doctor was the Chief of Cardiac Surgery at North Shore Hospital. He opened by saying "Mr. Starsia, are you the father of the lacrosse coach at Brown? He was very kind to my son at his camp and in the recruiting process. I saw your chart downstairs, have looked through the test results, you have a great doctor and he is prescribing exactly the right procedure. Tell you what, I will assist him in the surgery tomorrow." As you can imagine, this new information was a great comfort to my dad, who lived a long and healthy post-surgical life. I am forever grateful to this new doctor who was the father of Princeton attackman, Justin Tortolani. We had Justin as a camper at Brown and I had done a home visit during the recruiting process. I wished him well when he chose Princeton and while I may have felt, at the time, that I had not been successful, little did I know it may have been my most productive home visit ever! Justin went on to become one of Princeton's alltime players. He also became an orthopedic surgeon, trained in spine surgery and an expert in the field of terminal disc replacement surgery. Maybe you can still have a life if you don't come and play for me! I have run into Justin at a number of lacrosse functions and we always mention the story of having had our dads meet.

When I was inducted into the Legends Society at Lake Placid this past summer of 2018, my presenter was David White, my dear friend and college teammate and roommate. Dave is a Mohawk Indian from the St Regis reservation in upstate New York. During his remarks at the induction ceremony, Dave said that "lacrosse has been Dom's good medicine and he has shared it with the lacrosse world." I would say that, during my life in the game, I have tried. These two stories touched me deeply and certainly seem to have been influenced by some "good medicine." I wish for you that some similar tales grace your life, especially during this Season of Giving.

P.S.: In an incredible twist of fate, I heard from Justin Tortolani after this story was published and he and his dad recall vividly the meeting with Big Dom in the hospital. What puts all this into "Twilight Zone" territory is Justin's telling me that his wife Kim and Page Perriello were roommates and lacrosse teammates at Princeton!

# 50

# What's Next?

I can hardly believe that it has been more than a year now. It still feels as if my time as the Virginia lacrosse coach just ended a day or so ago. Surely the athletic director is simply going to recognize his misjudgment and I will re-assume my position.... Oh wait, the alarm just went off!

There is a quote of mine on the wall in the locker room at the new US Lacrosse Headquarters: "The wins and losses are fickle at best. It is the relationships that stand the test of time." I am here to confirm for you that the sentiment is true. If I coached my last college lacrosse game in April 2016, my career will have ended as the all-time winningest coach in Division I history, having won four National Championships and having been selected as the USILA National Coach of the Year in three different decades.

Still, I did not win enough.

I used to be guilty of saying quite casually that "the national championships are not that important, that it is how you treat people that marks the day." If Mike Pressler was nearby, he would always lean in quietly and say, "It's easy to say that when you have won a couple of championships" and, he is right. I learned to be more mindful of my language and subtly appreciative of the benefits that winning provides. While every piece of my life has been influenced by the arc of my coaching career, the relationships that clearly were enriched by the winning have stood even taller during these past 12 months.

Short of my dying, it is next to impossible to imagine a situation that would have the people I care about and who care about me talking to each other in a more meaningful way. It has been an unexpected blessing and it has been dramatically humbling to hear from so many of those I played with, those who played for me, my peers, my colleagues, fans of the game and, of course, family and friends. As coaches, we touch lives in a way that would be simply overwhelming to consider closely.

After having missed my oldest daughter's graduation from Columbia two days before the NCAA Semifinals in 2003, I was able to get to her graduation from Vanderbilt's Graduate Divinity School a month ago. I will have been to four weddings in these past seven months when I watch Zed Williams go up the aisle early in July. I visited every city and every school where Harlem Lacrosse has or will have a program by the Fall of 2017. What a joy to confer with all the young program directors and to see up close how lives are being changed with our game. I found time for coffee with Scott McWilliams, David Sloan, Julie Myers, Jim Stagnitta, Ryan Tucker, Greg Traynor and Mike Leahy. We did blackboard work with Jason Rostan, Ben Rubeor and Joe Thompson. I got on the field with David Jenkins, Andy Kay, Mike Murphy, Matt Poskay, Jon Torpey, Mikey Thompson, Colleen Shearer, Kevin Gates, Lloyd Carter and Casey O'Neill. I worked with the women's teams at Covenant School and Bridgewater College. I spoke with the men's teams at UPenn, Marquette, Cleveland St, High Point, Christopher Newport and Hampden. I found it liberating to be speaking with the players not as their coach. I could be frank and forthright.

I have written a number of pieces for various lacrosse publications. Why do I feel that compulsion? Are these stories that need to be told or, am I just talking to myself? I have appreciated the latitude of the editors and publishers who have allowed for some stream of consciousness but, where am I going?

Could I coach again? I feel great and somewhat energized by the time away. I painted the outside of my entire house with a three inch brush during the playoffs. It was strange to watch the teams and coaches in action, and it was probably at least as much a diversion for me as it was a homeowner's necessity. Why is it that professors get to take a sabbatical and it is never a consideration for coaches? In a profession that is almost life consuming, I think you might really benefit from six months away every 10 years or so. Spring 2016 was my 42nd consecutive year of college lacrosse. Many of you know that I have 32-year old twin daughters with special needs. Our lives were blessed when we found Innisfree Village, a wonderful Life-Sharing Community here in Charlottesville. The fact that we are not moving the girls nor leaving the girls limits my ability to consider any options away from this area.

If this is the end of my full-time active coaching career, what I have confirmed in these past months is of much greater significance than any personal anguish of not being able to write my serene ending and, it is this:

At the end of the day, you will truly be measured by how you treat those around you.

Thanks.

Maggie, Molly, Joe and Emma at Graves Mountain Lodge

Molly, Maggie, Joe, Emma and Daughter-in-Law Pam, May 2011

# Conclusion

When my wife overheard me say to someone about an event I could not go to because "I had to babysit the kids," she immediately stepped in and quietly corrected me, "You're not babysitting our children, this is our life." On another occasion, I overheard my son Joe, the first year he was on my staff, talking to one of the Virginia players and remarking "he talks to you guys the same way he talks to me at home." I cherish both of these moments because they reflect what I always believed about my life at home and at work.

I have always said that "I did not choose a profession, I chose a life." With four children under four, two with special needs, married to a brilliant, independent thinker and responsible for the behavior, performance and growth of 40 college undergraduates, I was too busy to separate out one from the other. I tried to live by a set of values that were the guiding force at home and in the locker room. There were lots of problems and rough spots along the way but, as often as possible, difficult decisions were made by a personal standard of "what is the right thing to do here?" If you can convince your players and your children that you have their best interests at heart, you have a chance of building the kind of relationships that will stand the test of time.

What I really came to treasure about coaching was the routine of it all and the daily exchange with the players and staff. I loved the anticipation of preparing for practice, walking into the locker room, the weight room and out onto the practice field. I was almost always the first one onto the field and can hardly remember a day when I was not excited to be there. We had a responsibility to be "on" every day and I never found that a chore. Even now, if I am working with a team for just one day, I have to control my excitement. I have often had to apologize to the head coach for yappin' at players I hardly know. I can hardly tell young coaches often enough that college athletes want discipline, they respond in a positive way to coaches getting after them on the field. They want a strong leadership presence with clear limits imposed fairly and consistently, without sarcasm and personal animus. You can set a relaxed and productive atmosphere in practice by giving confident players some good natured ribbing. In turn, I am not sure what I ever enjoyed more than having those same players give it back to me in a respectful manner.

Thanks again to all the players, who I will not begin to name. I was blessed to have been put in a position to influence some young men who I greatly admired. The key to success in the coaching profession…surround yourself with good people and create an environment where their talents can blossom and flourish. To all my assistant coaches, again, almost too many to name but without Mike O'Neill, Mike Caravana, Peter Lasagna, Paul Hooper, Mike Murphy, Hannon Wright, John Walker, Chris Colbeck, my son Joe and especially, Marc VanArsdale, none of this happens…thanks to you all. I could never repay adequately all the players, coaches, trainers, managers and staff who made coming to work every day such a joy.

I am presently involved in a number of different activities… some coaching at various levels and with men's and women's teams, working closely with the incredible folks at Harlem Lacrosse, coaching in the Premier Lacrosse League with Team Chrome, chairing some committees with the coaches' organization and with US Lacrosse and doing this writing. Some days on the practice field were better than others but I spent real time trying to imagine something meaningful to say to the team every day. I feel more and more that this writing may be an effort to satisfy the need that I have about my life continuing to have some consequence and meaning.

I thought about it recently in terms of trying to figure out what side of 66 (years of age) I am on. Am I still looking up at it?, trying to get better, trying to improve myself as much as possible? Or, am I looking back at it, trying to stay out of trouble and enjoy some quiet time? The answer is, "I'm a work in progress"…I do need to stay busy, I enjoy helping people, it's what makes me the happiest. At the risk of self-indulgence, I would suggest that my goal is to simply try and make the world a little better place, one small piece at a time.

With Maggie and Emma

# About Dom Starsia

Dom Starsia coached college lacrosse for 42 years, including 18 as an assistant and the head coach at Brown University and 24 years as the head coach at the University of Virginia. He retired from the college coaching ranks in 2016 as the winningest coach in NCAA Division 1 history.

Starsia had never seen lacrosse before he entered Brown University as a football recruit in the fall of 1970. He went on to be first team All-Ivy in both 1973 and 74 and was an All-American selection in both those years. Starsia played professional box lacrosse in the National Lacrosse League in 1975 and was selected to the US National Team that competed in the World Games in 1978. He was named the USCLA Club Defenseman of the Year in 1979 and was named to Brown's Team of the Millennium in 2000.

As a head coach, Starsia's Brown team won Ivy League Championships in 1985 and 1991. His teams at Virginia made 13 NCAA semifinal appearances, won 6 ACC Tournament Championships and 4 Division 1 NCAA Championships in 1999, 2003, 2006 and 2011. He was selected as the ACC Coach of the Year 8 times and won the Morris Touchstone Award as the USILA National Coach of the Year in 1985, 1991 and 2011.

Starsia was honored as the USILA Man of the Year in 2006 and received the organization's Frenchy Julien Service Award in 2017. He has served on the Harlem Lacrosse Executive Board since 2013 and received their Leadership Award in 2016. He received the Intercollegiate Men's Lacrosse Coach's Association Creator's Award in 2016 and the University of Virginia McCue Society Jim West Service Award in 2017. He was inducted in to the Lake Placid Legends Society in 2018.

Starsia has been inducted in to the Brown University, Rhode Island, New England and Central Virginia Hall of Fame. He was inducted in to the United States National Hall of Fame in 2008.

He presently serves as the head coach for the Chrome Team in this inaugural 2019 season of the Premier Lacrosse League.